Here is a book that tells you about
quiet woodworking—working outside
in the air of your backyard, cottage,
or apartment balcony.
Quiet woodworking is done with
hand tools, calmly and thoughtfully
at your own speed.
It is not "technical" and you
don't have to own a woodlot
or a mule.

There are projects to make
in this book—twenty-something—
but exactly how many and
what they are I don't know right now,
it's not important. There is one
real important project though,
and that's yourself.

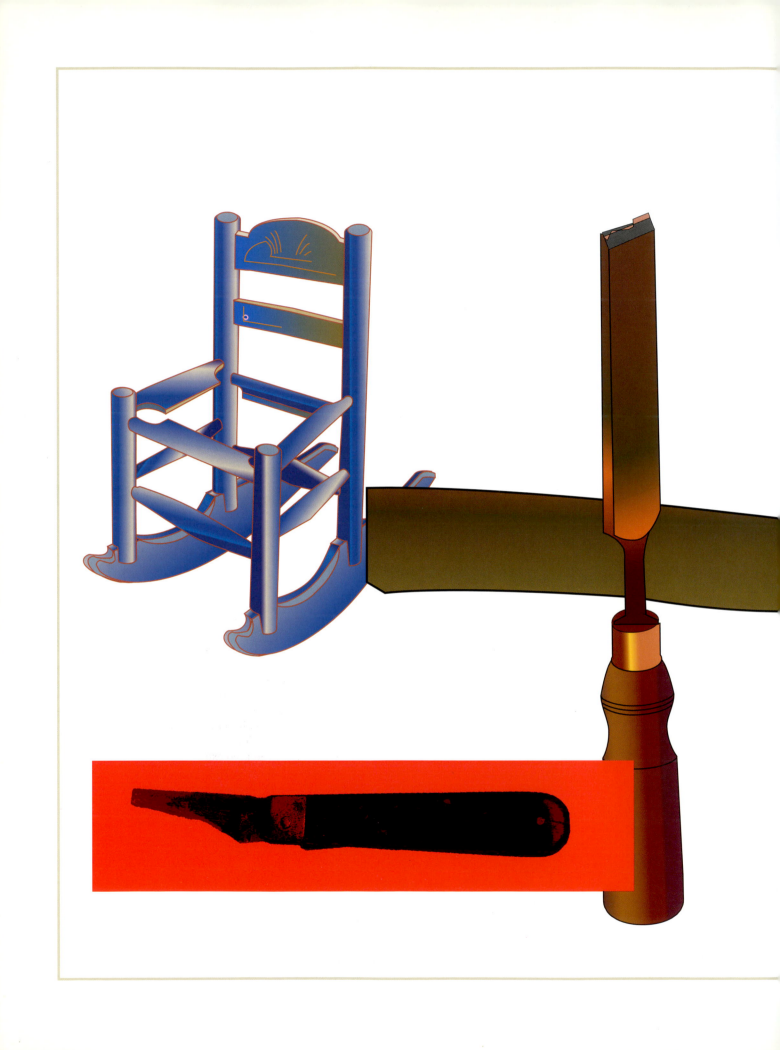

THE NATURE OF WOODWORKING

The quiet pleasures of crafting by hand

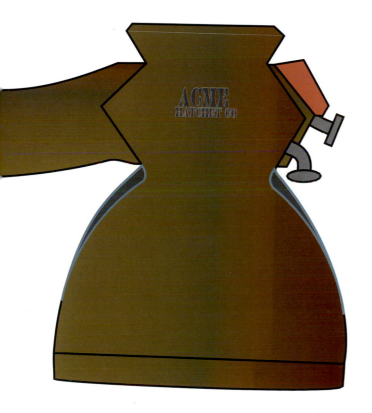

Lots of people have helped me and I'm only too glad to pass on what I know and, if I don't know something, I'll admit it.

If you were to visit me, you'd look around, I'd show you some things that I was proud of and some things that were goofy mistakes, and we'd probably get out some tool that I was fond of and we'd jaw a bit. I wouldn't expect you to pick up some tools and materials and start making something right away.

Later, you might come back and ask me how something or other has been made. Maybe you'd like to make one yourself.

I'd like you to treat this book the same as a visit with me. Browse a bit. Wander through the pages and back. If something catches your eye—look at it some more. If you need extra information, read what is written near it. Maybe it will tell you.

Come back when you are ready, your brain all prepared, and then we'll get started.

RODNEY FROST

Sterling Publishing Co., Inc.
New York

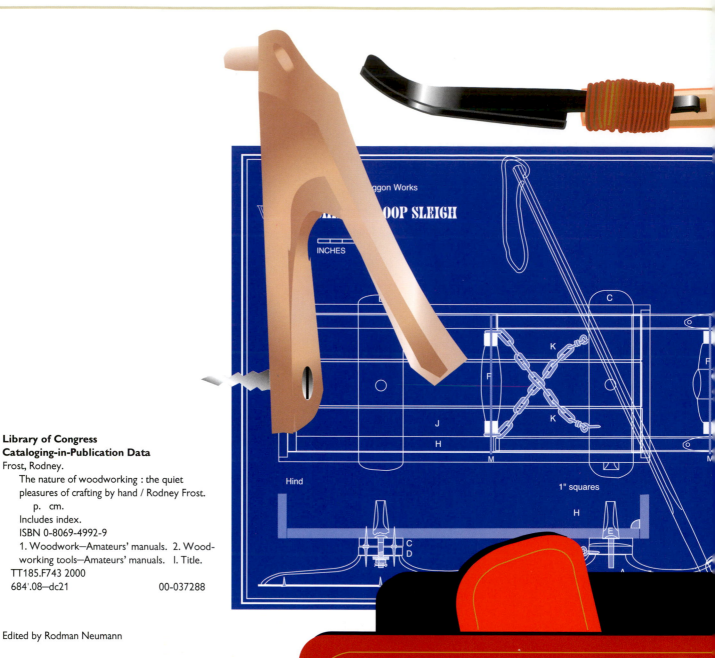

**Library of Congress
Cataloging-in-Publication Data**

Frost, Rodney.
    The nature of woodworking : the quiet
    pleasures of crafting by hand / Rodney Frost.
        p.   cm.
    Includes index.
    ISBN 0-8069-4992-9
    1. Woodwork—Amateurs' manuals. 2. Wood-
    working tools—Amateurs' manuals. I. Title.
TT185.F743 2000
684'.08—dc21   00-037288

Edited by Rodman Neumann

1 2 3 4 5 6 7 8 9 10

Published by Sterling Publishing Company, Inc.
387 Park Avenue South, New York, N.Y. 10016
© 2000 by Rodney Frost
Distributed in Canada by Sterling Publishing
C/o Canadian Manda Group, One Atlantic Avenue, Suite 105
Toronto, Ontario, Canada M6K 3E7
Distributed in Great Britain and Europe by Cassell PLC
Wellington House, 125 Strand, London WC2R 0BB, England
Distributed in Australia by Capricorn Link (Australia) Pty Ltd.
P.O. Box 6651, Baulkham Hills, Business Centre, NSW 2153, Australia
Printed in China

Sterling ISBN 0-8069-4992-9

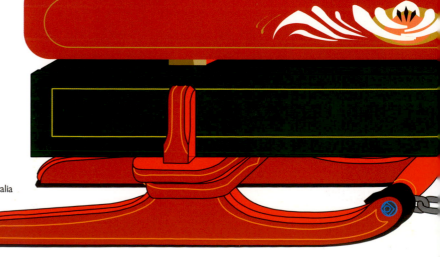

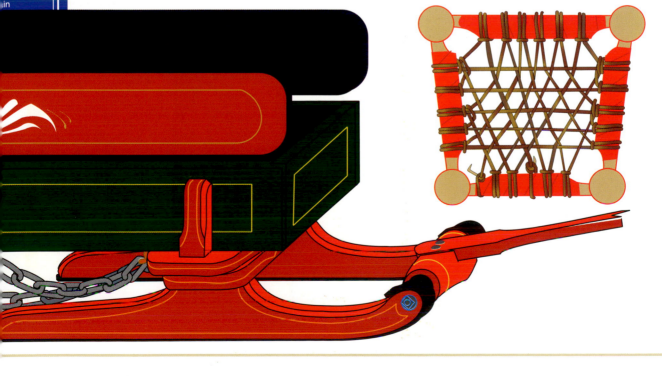

Before we begin, let me tell you something about how I've put this book together for you. The order of the projects and information that you might like to have about tools is not set out in the usual way—not the way that just about every other practical shop book presents its material. The fact is that people just don't learn the way "practical" shop books want you to learn. Try to teach yourself from one of them and you have a hard time. Sit down with a kid with a traditional woodworking book and before you get to page three—you're sitting alone!

I've been working at teaching myself woodworking since I was 10 years old. I had lessons at school (I seem to remember getting a certificate in it at one time in my teens) and I've made things for sale. Every so often I find myself in a classroom teaching. On these have I made this book.

On the other hand for those of you who just love to know what's coming up here's a list of what's in *The Nature of Woodworking*. But if you'd like *not* to read it—then don't—you won't miss a thing!

Contents

A Father of
A BOOK

Some of us, I'm afraid, come from a long line of people who, when they needed something done around the house, paid somebody else to do it. It's not that we had too much money, but rather we simply did not have the inclination, the tools, the know-how, even the courage to take on the project ourselves. In our efforts to overcome our disability, we would turn to magazine articles, books, and yes, even acquaintances, who would offer what they thought was advice. They would generally start by describing some expensive, high-priced electric gadget that was simply a must-have if we were to proceed with our plans. And even if we had said tool—which we did not—the next information they would pass on would invariably demand a level of mathamatical rigor not demanded of me since high school calculus, which I passed with 61 percent. Sometimes, we good-hearted, ham-fisted, under-tooled amateurs got the impression that all calloused, capable, and well-equipped woodworkers had signed a pact to keep us out of their club. And maybe they had—almost.

Except for workshop dads. A child in his or her father's workshop is a lucky child indeed, because no better wood-working school exists. Fathers don't talk down to watchful children; they explain with patience and care why they're applying a certain kind of paint or choosing a 120-grit sandpaper over a 180-grit, and they certainly don't demand that the pupil own any specific tools. It's enough that the child fool around with a hammer and some nails while watching the father work. All that, and fathers can dole out advice for everyday life besides.

The Nature of Woodworking is one father of a wood-working book.

I first met Rodney when he was a wheelwright in a tiny village called Mindemoya, which is smack in the center of Manitoulin Island, near the north shore of Lake Huron, in Ontario, Canada. A mutual friend introduced us, and told me that this eccentric-looking chap with the gray beard and paint-splashed overalls was really a Renaissance man. He was a graphic artist and at one point in his life designed the Gilbey's Gin bottle. He had also been an art teacher at the local high school on Manitoulin and reintroduced the local kids to their own art history. He was a musician, a father, a husband, a raconteur, and a pipe smoker. He wrote a column for the local newspaper. The space he had to fill each week was exactly one newspaper column wide and one-and-a-half inches deep. The title of the column was *Stocks Hill Scenic Route,* named for his neighborhood. The tiny space he had to fill, right in the center of the back page amid the real estate ads, could accommodate either 50 words or a small picture.

And although I never would have admitted it at the time, Rodney often said more in that tiny slice of newspaper than I did in all the stories and photos throughout the rest of the thing.

With Rod—a great respecter of tradition—there are no limits restricting how a person can create. As he reminds the readers of this book time and again, don't worry about making mistakes. Learn from them; but there are no woodworking police looking over your shoulder. Relax. Like a great chef who metes out ingredients with apparent nonchalance, Rodney knows the importance of accuracy, but also appreciates exactly what you're talking about when you measure things in *hairs, tetches,* and *quite a bits.*

A month before Rodney Frost finished this book, his father Fred Frost passed away back in England. He was 81. Though I never met the man, I knew that Rodney respected him deeply, and much of the philosophy that you'll find in these pages first—and I'm guessing now—came from Fred, who cast the mold for Rodney Frost's wonderful and refreshing take on woodworking, tools, life, love, and everything. From his home in Toronto, Rodney flew to England for the funeral. When he came back, although melancholy at his father's passing, he told me about some wonderful obscure old tools that he had come across and acquired on the trip. He found a s*omething-or-other, a widgidy,* and *a whatsit.* None of which would have come into his possession if it hadn't been for his dad. And when he talked about them, his eyes lit up like a kid's.

—*Peter Carter*
Senior Editor,
Chatelaine

When Peter Carter *was editor of* Harrowsmith Country Life Magazine, *he began suggesting that a book created by Rod would be worth having.* The Nature of Woodworking *is the result of that continual encouragement.*

Peter was born and raised in Northern Ontario and now lives in Toronto, where he works as Senior Editor for Chatelaine *(Canada's national women's magazine). Married with three children, Peter is a sensitive and sensible person. After studying journalism at Carlton University, he has worked on country newspapers and urban business magazines—the* Financial Post, Influence, *and* Toronto Business Journal *among them. He is co-author of* The Canadian Guide to Home Security, *published by Key Porter. As Editor of the* Manitoulin Expositor *he won the* Rolland Michener Award for Public Service Journalism.

The Home
TOOLBOX

If the places I've been are anything to go by, there isn't a house, home, apartment, or shack that doesn't have a collection of tools such as you see here. Throw in a few shoe brushes and tins of saddle soap, some plastic-handled thing you bought but never really worked, and maybe a dead paintbrush or two, and you could be anywhere in the world. This phenomenon crosses all class boundaries; it knows no distinction. We've all got them and, when something goes wrong, out comes the toolbox or junk drawer, and an attempt is made to fix it. But that's as far as it goes.

Most people will now be reliving the disappointed frustration that such memories kindle. There must be something more I can do with these things, you think, and in your heart you are a would-be maker, creator, artisan, one of them horny-handed, resin-smelling, pine-hewing folks. People who say with pride, "My granddad made this for me and better still he showed me how to make things for myself!"

This book will set you on the road to knowing a bit about some tools that will let you build in wood almost anything you can imagine. Using saws, spokeshaves, hatchets, augers, and draw-knives will become second nature; and here's something—you'll never use a chisel to open a can of paint again!

A quick glance over these pages will probably bring some familiar shapes to you. The ones I've colored sort of realistically are going to be useful to you in making the projects in this book. If you don't have some of them, or even if you don't have any of them, don't worry, I'll tell you where to get them and what they are for and how to use them.

In this book I'm not going to tell you a lot of names for things; it's not necessary to know what a tang or a ferrule is to be able to do nice work.

One time I was giving a demonstration of snowshoe-making to a group of teachers—well, they wanted to know the name of every little tool and gadget that I used. The problem was that I had made all the tools and gadgets myself to do particular jobs—jobs that I was familiar with, and I needed no names for them because I was working alone! After a while I was beginning to feel pretty incompetent having to say, "Don't know" so often and was getting ready to pack up and leave when I realized that knowing the names for every tool that ever was made wouldn't make me into a better craftsman—what's important is knowing how to use them.

I have come across a certain feeling in some people lately that they would like to know how to use some of these good old tools that are in the box and some of those at the hardware store. Somehow we have lost the knowledge and confidence to build a box to sit on or a tool to help you garden. The plain ordinary enjoyment and quiet contemplation of the whisper of wood shavings piling up around your feet—that's what this book is about!

How to
GET STARTED

Only one person in the whole world is capable of getting you started. Sure, someone can nag you and force you, they can cajole (what a lovely word) you, they can coax (there's another) you, but you are the only one that can decide.

I love working with wood and making things and everyday I get better at it, which makes it ever more enjoyable—but, when I have to get started . . . !

Here's what's coming up in the first section. Look it over carefully, no rush, if you're wearing a watch take it off and put it away, we'll be working in real time from now on.

How to make sawhorses that you don't have to show anybody but will be a great help when you're making things that are easy to appreciate.

How to drive, clench, and set nails—what to do when things go wrong and what clenching and setting mean.

Enrich your life by reusing tins that you like and so avoiding those annoying plastic containers that the stores always say are so handy but you know by experience are not.

How to use one of these things and what to look for if you have to buy a new one.

How to mark so that you know where you are going and which side is "up."

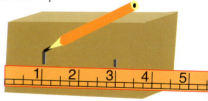

How to saw a little better than you can now.

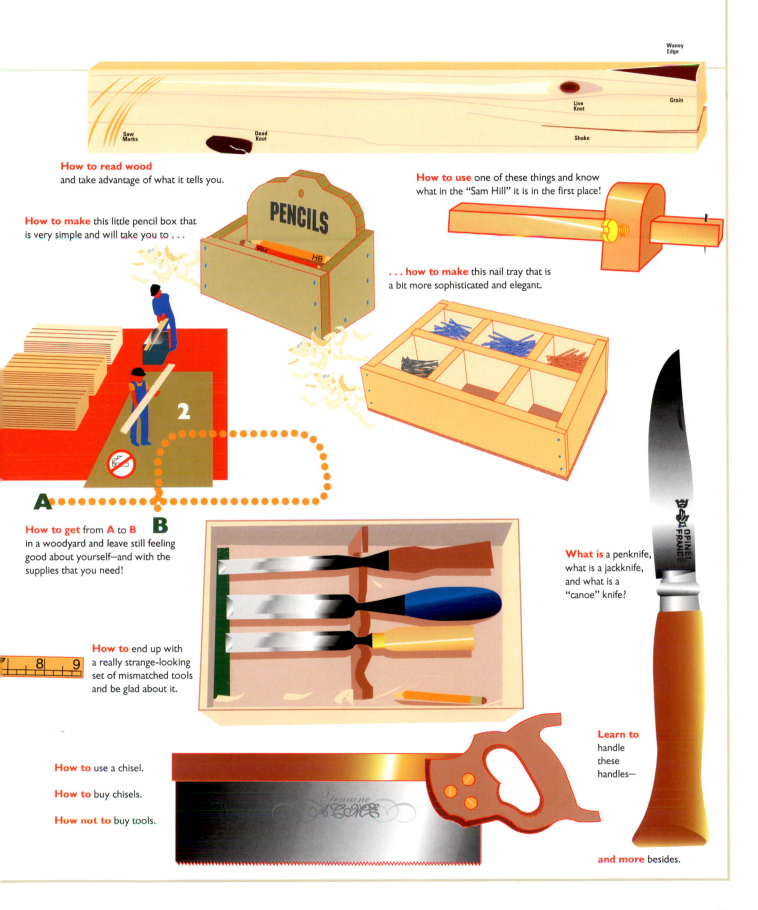

Waney
Edge

Grain

Live
Knot

Saw
Marks

Dead
Knot

Shake

How to read wood
and take advantage of what it tells you.

How to make this little pencil box that
is very simple and will take you to . . .

PENCILS

HB

How to use one of these things and know
what in the "Sam Hill" it is in the first place!

. . . how to make this nail tray that is
a bit more sophisticated and elegant.

2

A ● ● ● ● ● ● ● ● ● B

How to get from **A** to **B**
in a woodyard and leave still feeling
good about yourself—and with the
supplies that you need!

What is a penknife,
what is a jackknife,
and what is a
"canoe" knife?

8   9

How to end up with
a really strange-looking
set of mismatched tools
and be glad about it.

Genuine

OPINEL
FRANCE

Learn to
handle
these
handles—

How to use a chisel.

How to buy chisels.

How not to buy tools.

and more besides.

Some Simple
SAWHORSES

Quiet backyard woodworkers require little in the way of equipment. Cupboards, benches, dust extractors, drill presses—they don't need any of them! There are, though, a couple of pieces that make life a little easier; neither is expensive and they are nice projects to do. One is a pair of sawhorses and the other is a shaving horse. If you want to get set up at the weekend cottage or at your inlaws' place for a quiet weekend, you can build some there, too, and just carry your tools back and forth. On pages 48–51 you'll find an apparatus called a shaving horse that you can make; right now that may be a bit daunting, so our first project is to make the pair of sawhorses.

This is a very simple way of making sawhorses; later, you may find ways to improve them to your way of working.

The sawhorse is used for many more things than sawing.

Sawhorses are useful equipment for anyone; they can be used around the house to reach up and work high, you can put a board across to make a bench, they will support other projects, you can use them in the garden with a board for a picnic buffet, and so on!

Making a pair of sawhorses
You will need three eight-foot pieces of nominal 2 × 4 inch pine, cedar, spruce—whatever, it doesn't matter. A 2 × 4 is a very common size as it has been used for years in the building trade; cheap studs could be used for this project.

Start by marking the center of the long sides of the 2 × 4s, as shown at the top of the page opposite. Cut the pieces on the center mark so that you have six pieces, each about four feet long.

Put two aside; these will become the top bars. The other four pieces will become the eight legs.

The legs are at an angle to the top; so we will cut that angle with our crosscut saw. Measure, mark, and cut the four pieces of 2 × 4 (see **Figure 1**).

Lay one of the top bars on its side and nail on the legs at each end. Position the legs about two inches in from the end with the thick part of the taper lined up along the bottom of the top bar.

Nail together.

Mark and nail the gussets from scrap, as shown in **Figure 2.**

Done and well done!

Following the line
Watch the line on the top and the line on the side away from you. Do these first, then, letting the saw run in the cut and using it as a guide, gradually bring the saw down the back line.

Holding the saw
Everyone knows which end of the crosscut saw to hold, but many people have difficulty sawing straight. Here's the trick: Put all four fingers into the handle, and then bring out your first finger and lay it alongside the handle—POINT! This gives you the ability to control the saw.

Starting the saw cut
Put the saw blade on the line to be cut. Place your left thumb on the wood just left of the line (a vertical would tangent the end of your thumb) and touching the saw blade. Pull the blade back just a little (maybe two or

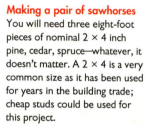

Once you are making the right sound, watch the line about an inch further on. If the saw starts to go off the line, gently increase the sideways

three inches). Do this a few times and, when you have a little groove started, push gently forward on the saw. Increase the length of stroke gradually until you are you are using almost the whole length of the blade.

Speed of sawing and pressure
When you are sawing, listen to your saw cutting the wood. Saw like your grandfather. Make the sound he makes and you will not be sorry. A good easy downstroke and a slightly quicker return.

The saw only cuts going forward, so do not waste energy on the back stroke.

hand pressure in the opposite direction until back on the line. Just before you complete the cut, reach over and support the sawn-off piece.

Take 3 pieces of 2 × 4 spruce, pine, cedar, or fir about 8 feet long. Mark the midpoint of the long side and cut off square.

Notice how the sawing feels different when you make these cuts. The reason is that you are now cutting with the grain.

It is quite difficult to do this cut. Don't worry if the saw gets a little off the line—we are not working to tight measurements. By the time you have made all four cuts, you will be getting the hang of it.

legs

legs   22"   22"

top

Figure 1.

Marking

Use a pencil for marking wood; do not use a pen. A good ordinary HB grade pencil is perfect.

Don't bother with the so-called carpenter's pencil; it's too fat for us!

When you mark off a measurement on the wood, put a small dash—not a dot. Try to make the dash accurately in the direction of the cut that you intend to make. When making rough cuts, such as those for making the sawhorse project, use a notebook or something similar to get the line square (at 90°). Later we will talk about using a try square for this operation.

Nailing the legs

Put the top bar on the ground. Hold a leg in place, square to it, and nail together. Two-inch spiral nails are good for this job.

Figure 2.

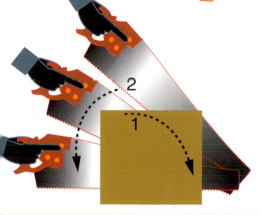

To do this project you might not have the materials just lying around. You may then have to take a trip to the woodyard. This can be a pretty scary event if you're not used to this; so turn to pages 18–19 for some confidence tricks!

Nailing & marking the gussets

Lay the board for the gussets under the slight overhang of the top bar. Mark and cut.

If you feel confident, nail first, then saw with your cross cut.

Notice how the legs are a little proud at the top—cut this off flush or, better, slope it off a bit to the outside. Use your saw (carefully) or trim them with your pocket knife.

Proud means a little bit taller or wider than the other piece when they are put together.

HAMMERS

Don't think that you have to be born knowing how to hammer in a nail—you can learn it, just like anything else that you need to know.

Most people who are not familiar with using a hammer think that you have to use a lot of force. This is just not so.

Imagine a hammer sitting on the edge of a table; it falls—onto your foot. How much force made the hammer fall? Almost none, just gravity. Did it hurt? You better believe it hurt! Yowee! Yet if no extra force becomes enough force to make you holler, where did it come from? From the movement and the weight of the hammer—that's where!

Same with nailing; let the moving hammer do the work. This is why hammers come in different weights. A four-ounce hammer feels a lot less painful than a one-pounder when it falls off the table!

Starting nailing

Place the nail on the spot that you want it to enter the wood. Gently hold the nail with your first finger and thumb. Carefully tap the nail into the wood using only enough force to move the nail a little at a time. When the nail starts to be gripped by the wood, take away your finger and thumb. Take your time . . . take your time.

To save fingers when holding a nail to start it, push the nail through a curl of wood or use a hair comb (though I can never remember where I last saw mine!).

Some people like to point their finger while starting.

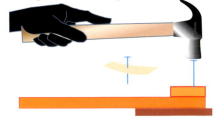

Claw hammer

Not just a stick with a lump of metal on the end, the hammer has some special features that are hardly noticable yet help you to use this basic tool with satisfaction almost every time.

The hitting face of a hammer is curved to help you keep the nail going straight.

Nailing

Hold the hammer by the end of the handle. A lot of people think that, by moving their hand up closer to the head, driving a nail will be easier. It won't and it doesn't. No matter whether you have small hands or big ones or if you weigh 90 or 250 pounds—hold the hammer by the end of the handle.

Practice holding the hammer. Get used to holding it properly.

Here's a little exercise to help you learn to hit the nail on the head . . . Put a thumbtack into a piece of wood. Holding the hammer correctly, position the face of the hammer over the thumbtack. Rest your knuckles on the same surface as the tack.

Without letting your knuckles leave the piece of wood, move the hammer up and down, striking the thumbtack.

Driving a nail is no different except that, because the nail is longer than a thumbtack, you will have to move your hand up a bit—the same distance as the length of the nail, actually. The action of the hand is the same.

The hammer does the work; all you have to do is guide it.

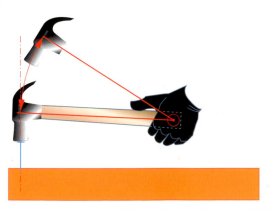

The handle is this long because then you get the most leverage.

Use the whole handle.
Use skill, not strength.

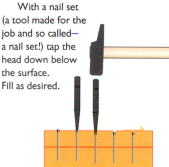

Hammers come in many shapes and sizes; they have evolved over hundreds of years to do this one job. Everyone that ever had to hit anything has had a special hammer for doing it.

Joiner

Cross pein

Ball pein

The other end of a hammer head is the part called the pein; it is what sets it apart from other hammers and does a special job.

Setting nails

Some nails have very small heads (e.g., finishing nails) and are meant to be pushed below the surface of the wood; then the hole is filled to give a pleasant finish (hence their name—finishing nails).

Here's how . . . Drive the nail almost completely into the wood—be careful not to hit the wood with the hammer.

With a nail set (a tool made for the job and so called— a nail set!) tap the head down below the surface.
Fill as desired.

Whoops, but hey . . . no problem!

If you've driven a nail right through the work and want to get it out, here's what to do . . . Turn the work over, and place it over the edge of a spare piece of wood or the edge of your bench, close to the nail head.

Strike the point down in the same way as if nailing, until enough of the head end is protruding for your claw hammer to pull it out.

Pulling out nails with a claw hammer can mar the wood surface.

To avoid this unpleasantness, put a little block of scrap wood under the head of the hammer as protection. If the nail is a long one, using a thicker block gives you better leverage besides protection.

When working on rough jobs or where a little more holding power is needed, using long nails and bending them over on the back is a useful method.

This is called clenching.

Clenching

Drive the nail through the wood. A scrap of wood under the work will protect the bench from the nail's protruding point.

Turn the work over.
Place a piece of heavy metal behind the nail head.
If the work is upright, a heavy hammer can be held behind the nail head.
With glancing blows in the direction of the grain, bend the point down. A final blow should be given to flatten the point into the wood.

Something of
WOOD

Wood comes from trees. There are two kinds of trees—those that are bare in the winter and those that are evergreen. Generally (and I do mean generally) the evergreen trees give us "soft" wood—and are classified as softwoods—and the others are hardwoods.

Walk into any woodyard and the main color that you see will be a light, whitish buff of softwood. This is because softwood is the usual wood in the construction trades. The jobs in this book are made from softwoods. The reason is that softwoods are easy (easier) to cut, they are easy to get, and they are less expensive.

The names of the woods are the same as the names of the trees that grew them. Spruce, pine, cedar, fir, hemlock are all softwoods. Oak, maple, birch are hardwoods.

You can tell the different kinds of wood in several ways. Color, texture, and smell are some of the ways. A good way to discover these is to go to a modern supermarket-type woodyard where everthing is labeled with its name—look and feel and smell. This last might cause a few glances in your direction, but don't be put off. Be like
a chef choosing vegetables—
a gourmet *chef du bois!*

Wood comes in standard sizes. These sizes are less than they appear. Here's why.

After a tree is felled, the bark is removed and it is sawn into planks one inch, two inches, four inches, and

Saw Marks

Dead Knot

Here is a typical piece of less expensive woodwarts and all!

I am giving you these names so that you can put them into—and sort of legitimize—your bargaining patter. Don't overdo it or the opposite effect will occur!

so on. The saws that are used are very big and have large teeth that scream their way through the log leaving great saw marks on all sides. The planks are dried, and as they dry they shrink. Then the rough teeth marks are planed—*dressed*—from them. Drying and dressing a two-inch plank means that now it is less than two inches thick, but it's still called a two-inch plank.

When you are at the woodyard (always take a rule with you) measure the thickness of a *nominal* one-inch piece of wood and you will find that it is about three-quarters of an inch. This is standard—you are not being ripped off!

Not al softwood is the same price. Wood is graded between the desirable and the less desirable. *Knots,* the remains of tree branches, are harder than the rest of the wood and lead to cutting difficulties; so wood with lots of knots or very large knots is cheapest. Planks with

Saw marks are left over from before the wood was planed smooth *(dressed)*. They have been left by the planer because they are deeper than the required thickness; i.e., the wood is thinner, so watch out if this could be a problem for you.

only a few very small knots or none at all are higher in price; this wood is called *select* or *clear.*

When you are buying wood, think about what you are planning to make. You can get a piece of knotty pine with a big knot at the end but clear and straight elsewhere for less money than a shorter piece of clear lumber.

Wood is a natural material; it moves around, twisting and turning as it dries or absorbs moisture. There are many names for these contortions, though commonly this twisting and turning is called *warping.*

There are two kinds of **knot**—live ones and dead ones. *Live knots* are generally brighter; in pine they are reddish, firmly embedded, and are a part of the wood. *Dead knots* are dark and gloomy, often loose and wobbly; they may be firmly set into a plank, but when you cut near them they fall out—they literally depart.

Woodyards are not the only source
Old furniture, packing cases, boxes, picnic tables, garbage, tree prunings, and wind falls are all treasures for the backyard woodworker—but watch out for nails and hardware that can ruin your tools!

Look out on garbage night, take a walk, know your territory as you would know your wood lot. Sometimes someone pulls down an old shed, someone cuts down a tree. Old furniture can provide some lovely pieces of oak, or other, nowadays expensive hardwood.
Go out after a storm and pick up the branches. I once made a bit of money from a sign and some knife handles that I made from a birch branch blown down at the pet hospital across the street.

Notice that the piece of wood above, even with all its faults, has a lot of clear wood for small projects.

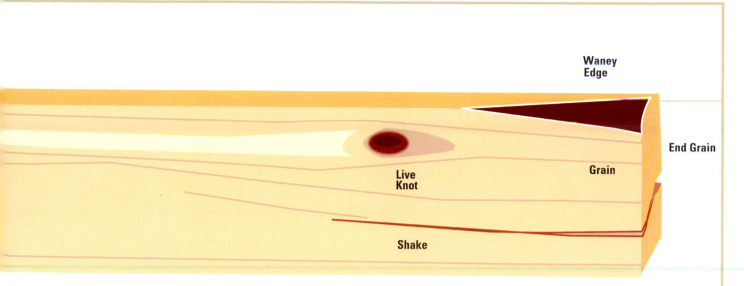

Waney Edge

End Grain

Grain

Live Knot

Shake

The *grain* is the exposed growth rings of the tree. When it is seen on the end of a plank it is called *end grain*. Grain has quite an effect upon the working of wood, especially when you are using hand tools. Most often the grain runs in straightish lines along the length of a piece of wood; sometimes it does not—then it is called *wild grain*.

Wild grain occurs around knot groups or when the tree has grown on a slope or had other difficulties. Splits in wood are called *shakes* or *checks*. Sometimes they go all the way along a plank. When you choose wood for your particular project, remember that one 8" plank with a shake is cheaper than two good 4" planks.

A *waney* (way-nee) *edge* is a bit of the outside of the tree, often with bark that is easy to see. Watch out for non-bark waney edges that can be all the way up one side. Sort through the select pile, and if you find any wanes, put on your "haggling hat."

Other kinds of wood

Wood comes in forms other than planks. Trees are mashed, diced, and sliced, and reassembled into sheets to save someone trouble and work later on.

Sliced-up wood that is stacked layer on layer with glue between to form sheets is called *plywood*.

Ground-up wood that is mixed with glue and rolled out is called *fiberboard* or *particleboard*.

The sheets are four feet by eight feet and range in thickness from a quarter inch up.

Reconstituted woods are hard to work with hand tools, but they are sometimes just what we need!

The garden tote and tool caddy on pages 76–79 make use of this recreated wood.

Wood sizes

Lumber is measured when it is sawn and those measurements stay with it! Most wood that you buy from the woodyard is smooth; it has been *dressed*—that is, a thin layer has been taken off (planed) to save you a lot of work. The piece of wood though is still called by the measurements that it had before, its *nominal* measurements. This means that a piece of "one-inch" pine is only three-quarters of an inch thick. Wood that is called 1 × 8 is ¾" thick and about 7¼" wide. These actual sizes are approximate because wood shrinks as it dries.

Standard sizes of wood

Actual Thickness	Actual Width	Nominal Size
¾"	3½"	1 × 4
1½"	3½"	2 × 4
¾"	5½"	1 × 6
¾"	11"	1 × 12

There are other sizes, of course; check them out. Lengths are generally in multiples of 4 feet, e.g., 4, 8, 12, 16. If you want a 7-foot piece, it's often cheaper to buy longer than have it cut. You will use the extra—sooner or later.

Wood labels

Lately retail stores for wood have sprung up all over. The setup is just like a self-serve supermarket, which takes a little of the romance away but gives you other advantages. Most of the wood is labeled with stick-on information. Just as in the supermarket, always check that the piece you have is the piece that belongs in that rack! Some new wood "outlets" pencil on the price—handy, but check it out because it may be the price of a longer plank from which some wood has been removed!

A Typical Label

This is a company name. Not to be confused with white pine, yellow pine, etc. →

Grade of wood →

Size of plank → (thickness in nominal inches, width in nominal inches, length in feet)

Bar code for the cashier →

Nelson Pine

Select

1 x 4 x 8

73 756 92 567

Visiting the
WOODYARD

Be friendly with your woodyard. Do not be intimidated by off-hand or rude remarks. They will either treat you as if you know nothing or assume that you know everything. You do not fall into either of these categories. You are someone who is learning woodworking and, unfortunately, like most activities it has its quasi-mysteries. These quasi-mysteries are only the jargon. You are learning the real mystery, which is how to do it! Be confident.

At your woodyard you will find quite a variety of people. Most of them are there to buy something that will help them to make a living. They will probably be deep in thought about what they are getting, how they will use it, and how they can buy economically.

Be courteous. Slowly you will gain confidence and you too will be thinking more about your project and the materials you need than about being in a strange place.

The Traditional Woodyard consists of three parts.

1 The office
2 Inside storage
3 Outside storage

Until you are familiar and feel easy around woodyards, the best way to get from **A** to **B** is by the approved route that woodyard operators prefer you to use.

Most areas of woodyards are physically dangerous. All areas of woodyards are psychologically dangerous.

Read and obey all signs in a woodyard.

How's how it works . . .

Start at **A**: Enter the building and go to the office, area **1**.

Give the person there your order. For example:

16 pieces 1 × 12 × 16 clear pine,
6 pieces 2 × 6 cedar, etc.

You will then be given a bill, which you pay. (So far you might as well be in a bank!)

You will then be given a receipt and a copy (generally yellow, don't know why)—some yards have a clipboard for this part of the ritual, at others you use the bare naked hand.

2

1 The office

Money changes hands here. Often the people that work in the office are strikingly similar in appearance. This can become extra confusing because some are friendly and others are offhand and surly. This would be easier to handle if behaviors were not erratic.

Be nice—always—and make the best of it.

Some offices are just a room with an antique adding machine and filing cabinet and a calendar from 1938. Others are more like a hardware store. Here you can buy paint, doors, tools, screws, nails, dowels, plumbing supplies, and so on. The main business, though, is wood; so check out the quality and prices of anything that is not wood.

You will often find specials in the office—drop by from time to time, even if you don't need anything in particular.

2 Inside Storage

Here is where the good wood is kept. Out of the weather. Later you will be able to walk around in here. Watch out for the sawyers. Be friendly and cooperative when they ask you to move—which they will, because this is a high-risk area.

Become familiar with the woodyard just the way and for the same reasons that in the old days one nurtured a relationship with one's butcher; i.e., not all cuts of meat

are the same, not all cuts of meat are tender or flavorful. This is the hardest part of beginning to work with wood; however, the situation will improve. Try to be diplomatic when you get your wood and see that it has waney edges, very large knots.

Discuss the wood and what you are looking for, but do not dictate—therein lies disaster and having to find another woodyard further away from home!

Take your paperwork to area **2**. The worker there takes the papers, gets the wood for you, and gives you back the white copy.

Proceed to **B**.

The main problem with this system is that you have to know exactly what you want, and you have to take what you get.

I suppose that to say that buying wood is rather like buying vegetables is not far off the mark, what with wood growing on trees and all. With this in mind—act accordingly.

Reminder

Woodyards are places of work. The workers and the customers are trying to make a living. They are serious and quiet. Buying wood is a private affair. Buying wood requires thought.

Specials

Lumberyards often have piles of odd wood on *special*. If you are looking for a good price for a simple project, look at the specials. When you see something good—buy *twice* as much as you need.

Often the specials are a really good deal. What happens is that someone at the mill makes a mistake or an order gets cancelled and the woodyard buyer gets a deal. The wood is fine; it may be just a few inches short of standard or a little thinner—something as simple as that.

Find out where the specials are kept; could be out front or maybe in some other usual spot.

3 Outside Storage

Wood for rough construction is kept outside. Watch out for guys carrying planks, trucks backing up, truck doors swinging open, piles of wood which could fall. Puddles. Sometimes there is a small planing mill and sawmill out in the yard. Interesting to see, but don't get in the way—and be careful.

Don't bother asking anyone working in areas **2** or **3** the price of wood. They do not know nor have they ever known.

A Handy
BOX

Everybody needs more boxes—and not only when you move house. I have made quite a few of these little containers and we always seem to find uses for more. They will travel well, and a box that was used for clothes pegs in the garden is now in the kitchen holding fliers for pizza specials.

Boxes are an end in themselves, but boxes are also transitional—they are for putting something in, and this something "completes" them. Should we say *complements* them?

Making this box

You will need a piece of 1 × 4 pine, cedar, spruce—whatever, it doesn't matter.

First mark off a line about a quarter of an inch to a half inch from the end. We do this because we want to start with a square end and, if the lumber is fresh from the yard, the end often has grit or damage or damp that will harm our tools.

Mark down the piece of wood for the bottom and front of the box.

The sides are marked using a straightedge "freehand" on the face (slope), but square on the edges.

Cut out the pieces using your backsaw. Be as accurate as you can, but don't be discouraged; later you'll get much better at it. You can use a crosscut saw, as you did with the sawhorses, though you will notice that the teeth of the crosscut saw, being bigger, will leave a more ragged surface.

For the back you need a piece of 1 × 8 wood. Cut this out just to length, and then cut out the shape in the order of cutting as shown. Keep the saw square to the front surface. These cuts will look a little rougher than you might enjoy, so sandpaper them smooth and round the corners.

Take the bottom piece and nail the back to it. Then put on the ends and finally the front. Drill a hole for a nail to hang it. **Use and enjoy!**

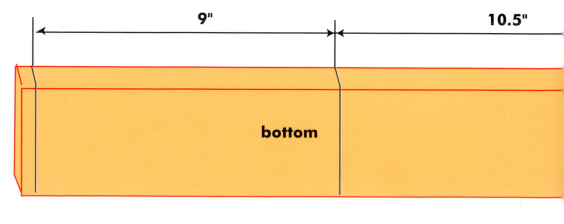

Starting the saw cut
Rest your thumb against the saw to help it start, drawing the saw toward you gently a few times.

Holding the saw
A light but firm and steady grip with—of course—the finger pointing!

Following the line
1 Watch the line on the top and the line on the side away from you.

Do these first, then—letting the saw run in the cut and using it as a guide—

2 Bring the saw back, still sawing to the almost-horizontal position.

Saw across and down the line close to you.

3 Complete the cut.

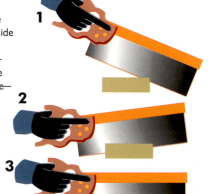

When cutting with a **backsaw** it is usual to cut right on the bench, rather than overhanging it as in crosscutting.

Push the wood against a stop—this may be part of the bench or fixed to the bench. Make the cut right through to the surface that the wood is sitting on.

Cutting the bench is almost unavoidable when sawing this way, so make suitable arrangements!

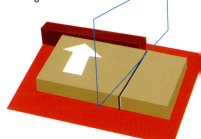

9"   10.5"

bottom

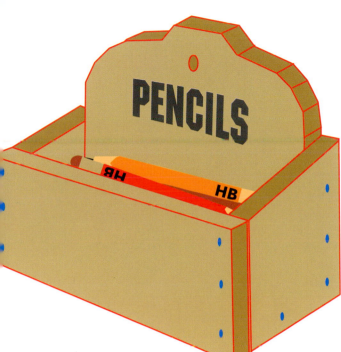

Marking the pieces for cutting

The cover of a book is fine for getting a cut roughly square, but for accuracy you need a **try square**.

The try square has a fat butt and a thin tongue—the fat butt rests against the edge of the wood. A **framing square** is one flat piece; so it does not help you perform this operation with ease or accuracy.

Put your try square on the piece as shown below, and strike a line with a pencil. Make sure that the butt side of the square is firmly against the side of the wood.

Now move to the other sides and continue the line. Be careful in your marking.

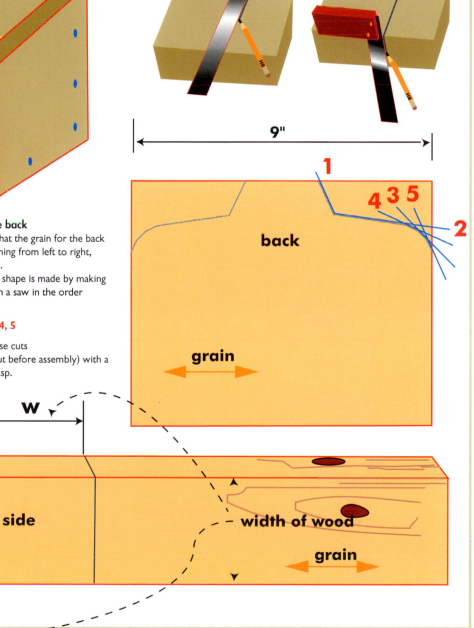

9"

back
grain

1 **4 3 5** **2**

Parts

Here we see the piece of 1 × 4 material laid out for making the box. The measurement "W" is the width of the wood—take this straight from a piece of 1 × 4 placed on top.

If you don't already have 1 × 4 scraps saved from previous projects, then cut off one or two pieces (e.g., bottom & side) and use them to mark "W". Keep scraps and off-cuts for later use.

Making the back

Make sure that the grain for the back piece is running from left to right, horizontally.

The top shape is made by making flat cuts with a saw in the order numbered:

1, 2, 3, 4, 5

Smooth these cuts out later (but before assembly) with a knife or a rasp.

4.5"   **W**

front | side | side | **width of wood**

grain

W

Assembling the Handy Box

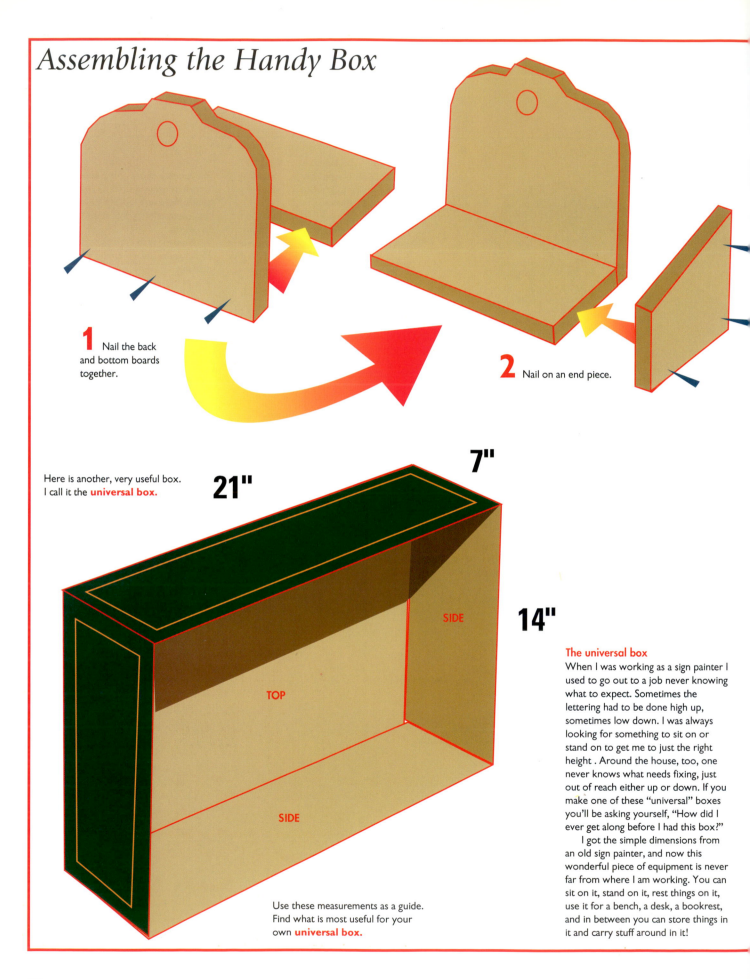

1 Nail the back and bottom boards together.

2 Nail on an end piece.

Here is another, very useful box. I call it the **universal box.**

21"

7"

14"

SIDE

TOP

SIDE

Use these measurements as a guide. Find what is most useful for your own **universal box.**

The universal box

When I was working as a sign painter I used to go out to a job never knowing what to expect. Sometimes the lettering had to be done high up, sometimes low down. I was always looking for something to sit on or stand on to get me to just the right height . Around the house, too, one never knows what needs fixing, just out of reach either up or down. If you make one of these "universal" boxes you'll be asking yourself, "How did I ever get along before I had this box?"

I got the simple dimensions from an old sign painter, and now this wonderful piece of equipment is never far from where I am working. You can sit on it, stand on it, rest things on it, use it for a bench, a desk, a bookrest, and in between you can store things in it and carry stuff around in it!

3 Nail on the other end piece.

Joints

In making this box you are making butt joints. This is a common joint known by just about everyone. There are more elegant ways to join at the corners we will learn them later.

4 The front piece is nailed on last.

5 A nice finesse is to slice off the wood on the top-front edge of the front of the box to continue the slope of the sides.

In the picture on the opposite page you can see that my measurements for the **universal box** are 7" × 14" × 21".

Close is okay. Cut the top from plywood; a half inch thick is good. Cut the two long sides 21" × 6½" (to allow for the top, but this is not at all critical—you could make it 7" and easy to remember).

The ends have to be a little shorter to fit between the sides (get this measurement as you work). Nail it all together, or if you feel fancy use screws. Glue if you wish. Paint it and feel right at home.

The Handy Box is complete.

SAWS

Most woodworking tools are for cutting, and each has its own primary use. Crosscut saws are made for cutting across the grain of wood. With all saws the number of *teeth*—or *points*—determines how smooth your cut will be. The more teeth per inch the saw has, the smoother the cut.

A good crosscut saw to get is one with about nine points per inch. There are many excellent saws on the market—buy what you can afford, but remember the cheapest tools are the most expensive! One that will last for years won't cost much.

Starting a cut
Rest the saw on the side of your finger and thumb, and pull back a few times. When it's started— go to.

Underway
Put a little pressure on the saw and push forward. Watch the line on the top and far side. Keep your finger pointed! The saw only cuts going forward; the back stroke does not cut. Rest while doing the back stroke!

When sawing, get the saw to make the noise that your grandfather makes while sawing. Quiet and easy . . . zzzt (forward), aahhh (back) . . . zzzt, aahhh . . . zzzt, aahhh.
Be cool!

When buying tools, hold them and get the feel of them; point your finger when holding the handle, and make sure it feels good for your hand. Plastic handle or wood handle; it's your choice.

Set
Saw blades are not flat; the teeth stick out on either side. This is called the **set**. The set help the saw cut without sticking by making the cut a little bit wider than the blade.

If your saw tends to go off to the left or right, no matter how good you are becoming, it could be that the set is wrong. Check this out in a book or with a sharpening expert.

Saw teeth

Crosscut & Tenon   Rip

Set

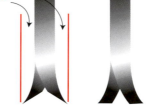

Saws that stick
When you are working with twisty or greenish wood, saws can stick. I rub a bit of candle wax on the sides of the blade if this happens. Pickling wax (paraffin) works well—keep some handy with your tools.

Ripsaw
A saw that can easily be mistaken for a crosscut saw is called a ripsaw. The difference is in the teeth. The teeth of crosscut saws are pointed, but the ripsaw has teeth that are like little chisels. A good indicator is that the ripsaw has **fewer** teeth to the inch, sometimes only four or five.

The ripsaw will not cut at all well across the grain; it is made for ripping long planks, lengthwise—along the grain. You may come across a ripsaw when buying at yard sales or flea markets.

Backsaws (sometimes called *tenon saws*) are essential to woodworking. Your tenon saw becomes so familiar after a while that its handle just fits your hand like the handshake of a trusted friend.

When buying a backsaw, really take your time and really feel it in your hand. If it feels too heavy, look for another one. If it feels too long and awkward, it's probably too long for you.

Backsaws come in different lengths: 8", 9", 10", etc.

I find that a 12" is most useful for general work. Remember that you hope this tool will last for many years; so get one that you really like. The backsaw is called a backsaw because, unlike the crosscut saw, it has a stiff back to keep it rigid and make straight cuts. It is called a tenon saw because in the age-old tradition of most trades a tool is named for what it does—in this case, making tenons. Tenons are part of a wood joint that you'll soon be making.

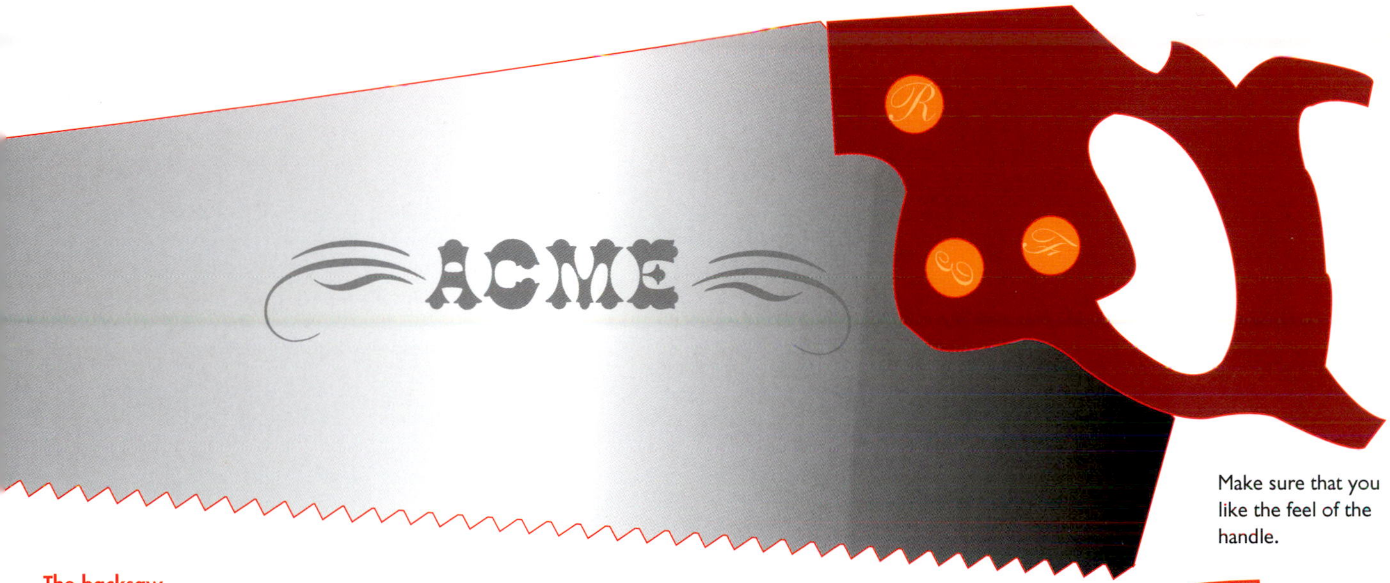

ACME

Make sure that you like the feel of the handle.

The backsaw
The back of a backsaw is sometimes brass and sometimes some other metal.

These bolts hold the blade and the handle together. If the handle is wobbly, tighten these.

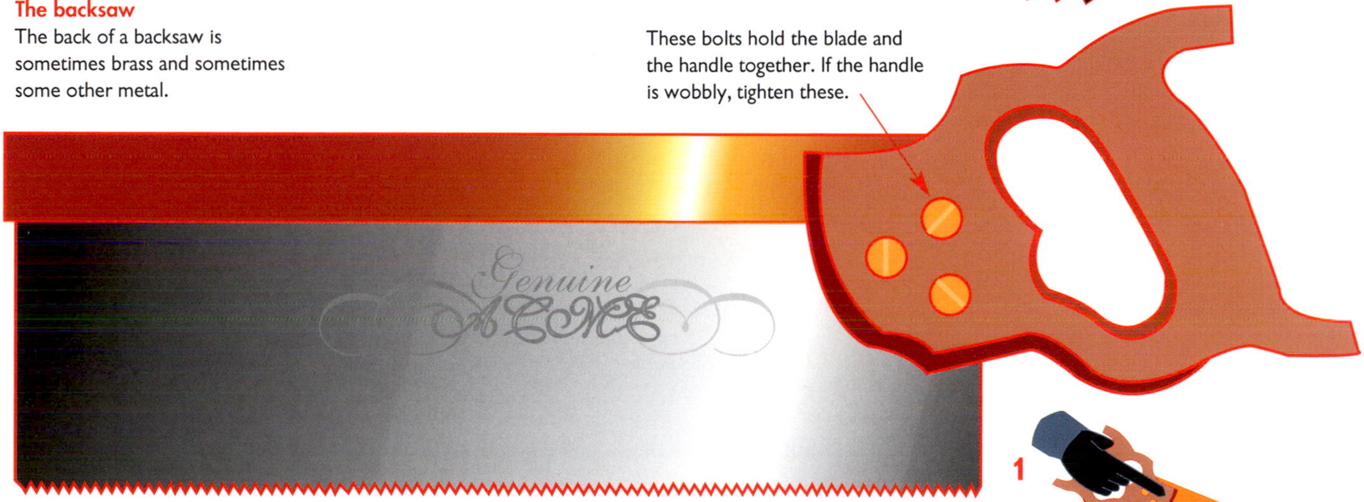

Genuine *ACME*

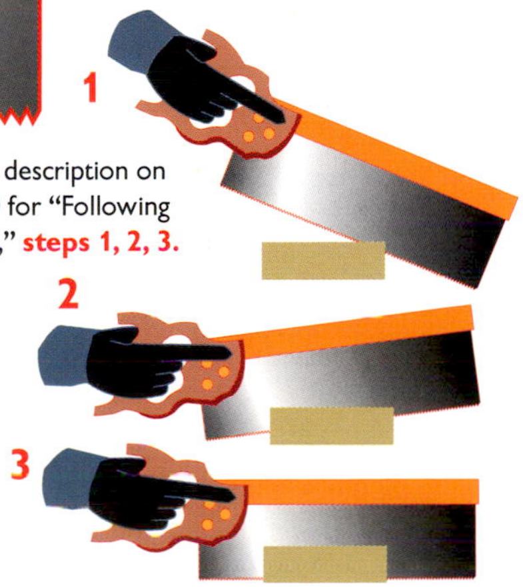

See the description on page 20 for "Following the line," **steps 1, 2, 3.**

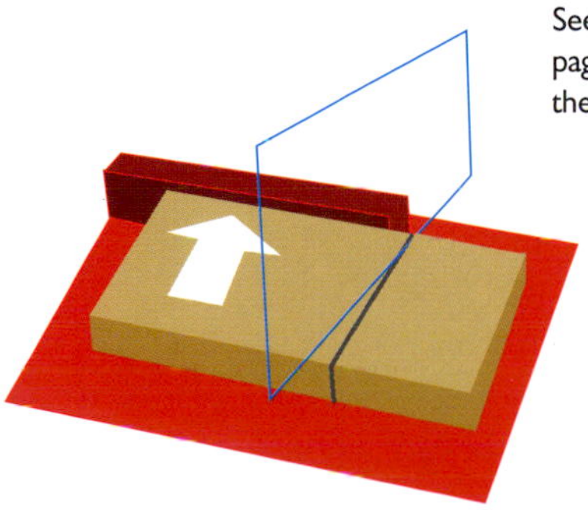

1

2

3

Keep your finger **pointing** when using the backsaw. Most of the problem people have with sawing "straight" is because they don't point.

Use a **stop** to push your work against. The saw generally goes right through; so put a piece of waste wood on the bench if you don't want to cut it.

For working in the garden, you might want to make a one-plank bench with a stop at one end and put it on your sawhorses.

After the bludgeon or mallet, I suppose the most primitive tool that we have is the knife. Unfortunately the word *primitive* has come to mean merely crude, unweildy, or, at best, naïve. I use the word primitive in its true sense, that is, *of the first* (as in prime), *primary* (as in primary objective).

Like any other tool or machine, a knife is only as efficient as its operator; so respect the humble knife.

For the work in this book, it is good to have a little knife of some kind: a folding knife, a pocket-knife, or a penknife.

Many people call any folding knife a jackknife; I don't because a jackknife, to me, is a specific kind of folding knife; it has a heavy blade and a spike. Boy Scouts used to have jackknives, and people always said that the spike was the thing for getting stones out of horses hooves! This is not exactly true; some jackknives do have a hooked spike on them for getting stones out of horses' hooves, but the straight spike on most jackknives is for use in splicing ropes—something that sailors used to do a lot.

Pocketknives seems to describe small folding knives that go into and are kept in your pocket—and why not? Those of us, who like quaintness and are happy to be the carriers traditions that add a bit of richness to life, call them *penknives.*

Penknives were once needed to sharpen quill pens; they were also used to hold the parchment down to stop it sliding around while you wrote on it.

On the opposite page is a picture of a knife (labeled "EXACTLY AS SHOWN") that I found in a bunch of old tools someone was throwing out. I applied one of my favorite sayings to it, "Looks bad but I think we can fix it," and fixed it. However, I soon found it to be too much like some-one else's cast-off shoes and looked for one that was a little less mature! I retired this old soldier to my chalkbox—and there it remains to this day, sharpening sticks of chalk into a chisel point and resting in between.

I bought an *Opinel*™ *French peasant knife;* it works beautifully, andb has a nice curve on the front end of the blade and an unpretentious, no-nonsense wood handle. I thoroughly recommend it! The Opinel™ knife is not expensive and it comes in various sizes. The small one is quite as big as anyone would need. If you are planning to "defend the Alamo," get the next size up.

Make your own knives

Knives can be made by you in your own backyard with almost no equipment that you don't have already.

Holding a crooked knife

The advantage of the **crooked knife** comes from the extended thumb.

Put out your hand, palm up, fingers and thumb extended. Place the handle of the knife across your palm, the cutting edge of the blade toward you. Curl your fingers around the handle. Close your thumb onto the handle—don't curl it around your fingers as in the traditional dagger hold; leave it upright, moving it away from you until it meets the handle. Notice how the handle is shaped to accomodate the thumb.

Sharpening of knives

Knives are sharpened, by me, in one of two ways. Both ways are good and have their advantages.

Flat sharpening — this is when you bevel both sides of the blade. Some knives, with thin blades, have to be sharpened this way. Probably the most usual method for many people.

Chisel sharpening — I like to sharpen my knives flat on one side (the back) and beveled on the other. This method is easier to touch up when the edge needs it. I like the way one has a choice with a chisel edge— you have two cuts with one tool.

A good folding knife with two blades can be sharpened one blade flat, the other chiseled!

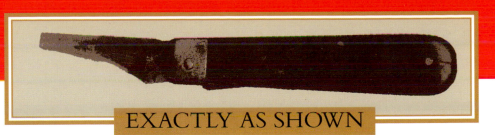

The Opinel knife

What a great knife! It's not expensive, holds an edge, and has a device to stop the blade from folding back on your fingers; it has a no-nonsense wooden handle, a nice shape, can be ordered by mail or bought in person, and comes in several sizes. (The small is shown here at actual size—so if you're after bear or are into "jungle warfare," buy the next size up!)

Crooked knives

The **crooked** in crooked knives comes from the fact that they have handles and blades that make them easy to use with the blade toward you. This is a much more controlled way of cutting—a bit hard to get used to, perhaps, but well worth the effort.

The **crooked knife** above I made from a file. The handle is a piece of antler inset with copper nails. The blade is fixed firmly into the handle with resin from a pine tree. This knife is sharpened like a chisel, i.e., flat on one side, beveled on the other.

For use with the left hand, make a knife exactly opposite to this—hold the page up to a mirror.

Canoe knives

Crooked knives that have a turned-up end are called **"canoe" knives** (at least by me and a few others). The purpose of this upturned blade is that this makes it useful for getting into tight spots and means that it can also serve as a whole kit full of gouges. Working in the middle of a plank is easier with a canoe knife than with a straight knife—crooked or not!

The knife below is made from a file bound on with leather strips. Some folks use brass wire. The handle is a piece of birch branch selected especially because of its shape and then modified a little.

A Front Porch
PEST SCARER

Surely there can be not one among us who at one time or another has not wished that something natural in this world, town or country, were not here! The massive seagull that eats the food put out for your tremulous sparrows, the cat who is, even as we speak, deciding on your flower bed, the squirrel who manages to find a secure foothold even on that complicated slick-surfaced baffle guaranteed to keep him off the wild bird mix. Shouting, whistling, waving arms, firing cap pistols★ can be as physically disturbing as the mental irritation already looming large without. Be refined—make an elegant pest scarer. Use it!

★ Believe me, I know a genteel lady who keeps a cap pistol on her window ledge for just such a purpose. The time that I sat pleasantly chatting on a summer afternoon, quietly taking tea with her and she jumping up and firing a few shots through the screen window, prompted me to comment that I had actually wondered as to its incongruous presence.

To be on the safe side, rest the wood on a bench or secure plank. Put the knife blade on where you want to split.

NOTE: It is important to split off, cleave, or *rive*, as it is correctly called, the pieces—not saw them.

Grain

A

Making the pest scarer

Only a knife and a drill are needed for the whittling-stick pest scarer and noisemaker. (Well, you do need a saw to start, but to tell you this makes it sound more complicated than it really is!)

Take a piece of kindling wood that splits easily (cedar or redwood, for example). Cut a piece about 7" long and split off a piece about 2" wide. Split it into three pieces of the proportions shown.

Shape part **A** by rounding the ends and smoothing its surfaces.

Mark the centerline, and on it at one end drill a hole about 5⁄16" diameter. Drill three holes 1⁄4" diameter on either side of the centerline, as shown in the pictures above.

Now put your knife at the middle of the end and rive (split) it into two roughly equal parts.

Part **B** is what I call the paddle. Mark it out as shown and whittle away the waste (saving the long bits from the side for making the pegs).

The top and bottom of the paddle have to be a little smaller than the large hole in part **A**; so keep checking the fit as you work.

Then tap it down with another piece of wood—not a hammer!

When splitting wood, remember your other hand—don't get it in the way of the knife.

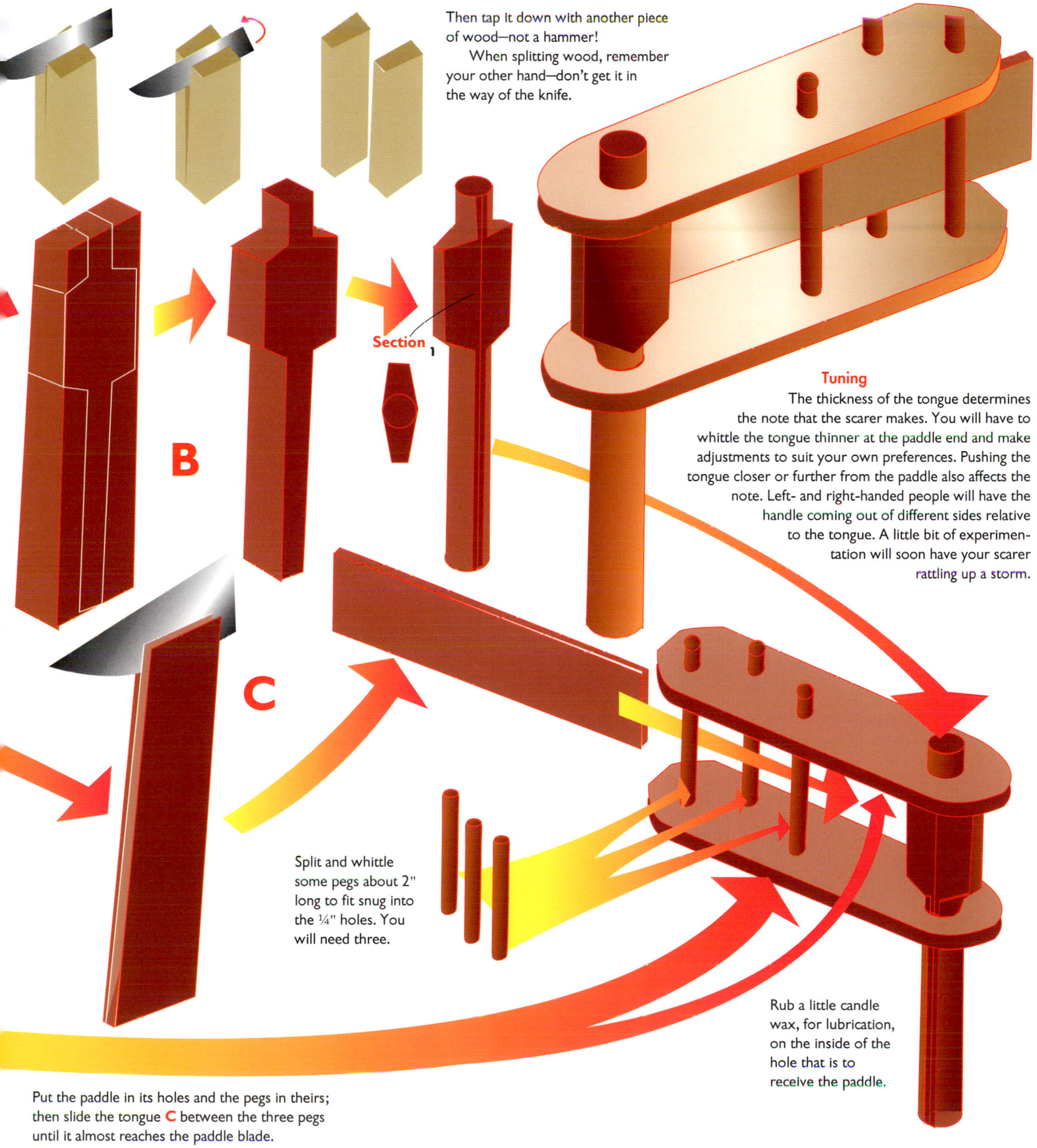

B

Section 1

C

Tuning

The thickness of the tongue determines the note that the scarer makes. You will have to whittle the tongue thinner at the paddle end and make adjustments to suit your own preferences. Pushing the tongue closer or further from the paddle also affects the note. Left- and right-handed people will have the handle coming out of different sides relative to the tongue. A little bit of experimentation will soon have your scarer rattling up a storm.

Split and whittle some pegs about 2" long to fit snug into the ¼" holes. You will need three.

Rub a little candle wax, for lubrication, on the inside of the hole that is to receive the paddle.

Put the paddle in its holes and the pegs in theirs; then slide the tongue **C** between the three pegs until it almost reaches the paddle blade.

A Simple
CLACKER

When we were a rural people, we used to need clackers to keep the crows from the corn. I don't know what they use now, but I know that sometimes people want to make some kind of a noise that's more piercing and less throat rasping than a human holler.

Kids love these just as much as grown-ups get annoyed by kids using them. As a woodworking project it may seem somewhat simple, but I've seen these things carved and turned so beautifully I believe that what they lost on the roundabouts they for sure gained on the swings!

Clackers have no limits; you can make them big, you can make them small—real small. When you've made one you can make another.

Practice your whittling skills, your chamfering skills; no one is gonna say, "Well that doesn't look like any clacker that I ever saw!" And if they do—great! And later when you are just one of the most happy and quiet backyard woodworkers on your street, you will be able to say, "I owe it all to clackers, that's where I got my start!"

Making a clacker
Get a flat stick. Mark it into three pieces as shown.

Drill two holes in it at one end of each piece.

Tie the two short pieces, one on either side, with a string, bootlace, or strip of cloth.

Using the clacker
Hold the long end of the stick. Wobble the two pieces on the end rapidly back and forth!

Tools to use
Various tools can be used to make this clacker. Be as high-tech as you want, as long as you don't disturb other people.

This project can be done over and over again using different tools—let's see, you could use:

- just a penknife
- a draw knife, a penknife
- a draw knife, a saw, a drill*
- a spokeshave, a draw knife, a penknife
- a spokeshave, a draw knife, a penknife, a saw
- a spokeshave, a draw knife, a penknife, a saw, a drill
- a spokeshave, a draw knife, a saw
- a jigsaw*, a drawknife
- a jigsaw, a penknife
- etc.

* Power tools are really easy to use; they do save effort—sometimes, just as cars do—and they require the same kind of responsibility.

To the right here is a good idea for this job and any others that it can apply to. Make all the parts together and then cut them apart.

By doing it this way, it's easier to control the pieces because there's something to hang on to while you work. Some parts have to be done after they are separated—but that's not a problem.

A Nail TRAY

Elegance is not just *pretty* and *acceptable*. Elegance, like beauty, is useful.

Putting two pieces of wood together can be done by just butting them together with some kind of fastener, as we did with the Handy Box on pages 20–23.

If we want a *more elegant* corner, we can do it by making one of the pieces thinner at the end and then fastening them together.

If we want a *stronger* corner, we can do it—by making one of the pieces thinner at the end and then fastening them together. This is called a *rabbet* or *lap joint*.

Beauty—eh?

Making a nail tray
Mark and cut the long sides and nail together using 1½" finishing nails.

Mark the bottom of the box on a piece of plywood or masonite. Put your tray frame on top of the marked-out bottom, and **eyeball** it to check that you have it right. Cut out the bottom using the crosscut saw at a low angle (to avoid making too many splinters on the other side). Nail the bottom to the frame using 2" spiral nails. Smooth any rough edges with sandpaper.

Cutting shoulders
Place the wood firmly on your bench. Hold the piece against a stop and saw the shoulder.

Go down the far side to the line, and then carefully bring the saw back to horizontal. Saw down the line nearest to you; using the cut that you have done so far, guide the saw.

The rabbet or lap joint
The **rabbet** or **lap joint** is a little stronger and more refined than a butt joint. The Handy Box that you made (on pages 20–23) can be redesigned to use this joint. **Try it.**

NOTE that the rabbet joint is cut only on each end of the long sides.

Getting started
There are only two measurements to start—the sides and the ends. Mark them on a piece of 1 × 4 wood. When you have cut the pieces, measure and mark the shoulder lines.

The **thickness** of the wood **(t)** will tell you how far down they should be. Don't be embarrassed to lay the wood thickness on the line to get or to check this measurement. This is called **eyeballing.** With practice your eyeballing will become as accurate as you will let it.

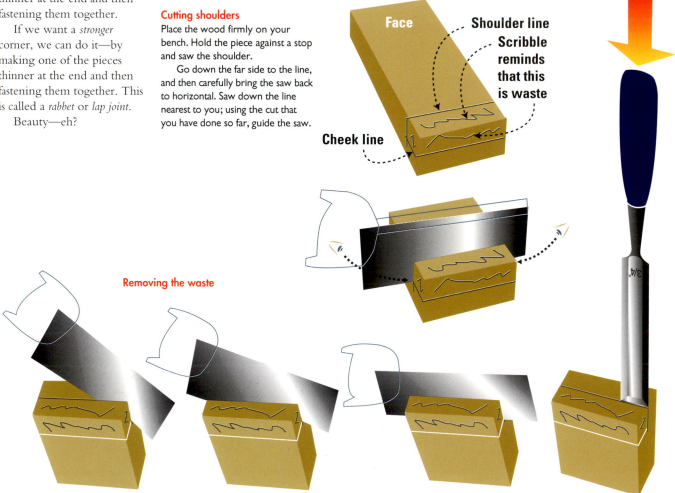

Face **Shoulder line**
Scribble reminds that this is waste
Cheek line

Removing the waste

Using a saw
Secure the wood upright, and saw down using the same method as when cutting shoulders. The sawing will feel a bit different (more slippery) because you are going with the grain. Be careful to stay on the line. This is difficult because the grain wants you to go its way.

Using a chisel
Place the wood upright, and put the chisel on the line. Strike down on the handle with a mallet, or with the side of a hammer.

Checking for squareness

Before you put the frame on the bottom to mark for cutting, check the squareness. A try square can be used for this—and/or measure from corner to corner diagonally.

When both diagonals are the same length, the box is square.

To adjust the squareness a little, push on opposite corners.

Marking

Mark the position of the shoulder line with your try square just as when you mark for cutting out. Halfway down the side, mark a line parallel to the face and carry it around the wood over the end and down to the shoulder line on the other side. On the next page you will be using a special tool for this kind of work called a *marking gauge*.

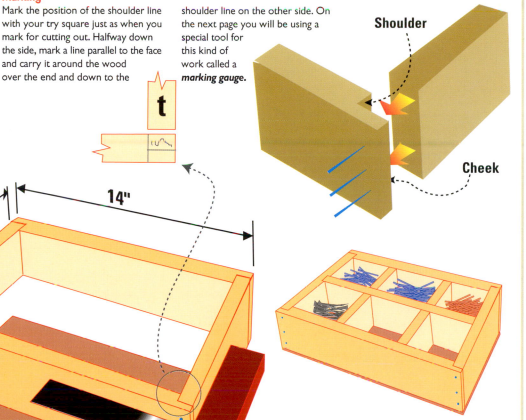

Shoulder

Cheek

How the crosspiece dividers are made is on the following two pages.

Nails for a nail tray

Little pieces of metal that are forced between the fibers of wood are called *nails.* For woodworkers they are really just a temporary holding device.

Did you ever notice the respect that some folks have for things made without nails or screws? I think the adulation is a bit overdone, but it is a good feeling not to have to rely on temporary fasteners.

Finishing nails have small heads on them and are often set into the wood.

Spiral nails turn like screws when they are driven into the wood, and so give a good grip.

Paring

If the cheeks are not smooth and accurate to the line, they can be leveled by *paring*.

Holding the chisel flat (on the same plane as the cheek), push the chisel across the check to level it. *Do not tilt the chisel.*

Keep your other thumb on top of the chisel to help you keep the chisel level and flat.

The waste wood will split off if your saw cut is accurate. If the waste does not fly off, check that the saw cut does in fact form a straight line between the marks on both sides. Resaw the shoulder and proceed.

Assembling the Nail Tray

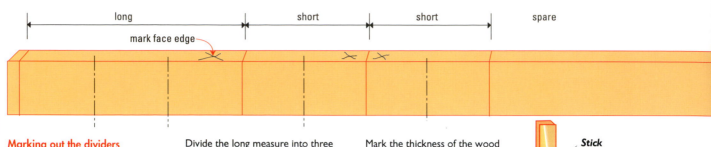

long | short | short | spare

mark face edge

Marking out the dividers

Strike off along your wood the three pieces that we need for the partitions. The two short pieces are the short inside measurement of your box, the long piece is the long inside measurement.

Divide the long measure into three parts. Divide the short pieces in two.

Mark one edge of the wood with an **X**. We will call this the **face edge**.

From the face edge measure halfway across the width of the wood and strike off on the dividing lines.

Mark the thickness of the wood straddling the dividing line. Take the mark across the edge and down the other side. Strike the halfway mark on these lines. Scribble the waste. These will be the **slots**. **NOTE** how the slots are on different edges of the board.

Stick

This is a marking gauge.

Sliding stop
Screw
Point

Cutting the slots

With a backsaw cut down the lines that mark the slots. Cut in the same way that you cut for the joint at the box corners. Be careful not to go further than the center scribed mark.

When cutting, cut on the **inside** of the line. This may sound a bit precise to you right now, but it **can** be done—and by you.

Lay the wood on a firm, flat surface with one of the slots facing you straight on. Place a ¾" chisel* on the centerline with its bevel toward you. With the chisel is perfectly upright, hit the end of the chisel handle with a blow downwards, driving the chisel about ⅛" to ¼" into the wood.

Pull the chisel out and move it toward you a little—maybe ⅛". Incline the top of the handle toward you very sightly, and then give the handle a blow at the inclined angle. The bevel will take the chisel in toward the first cut.

Repeat this until you are halfway through the plank. Turn it over and do it again.

* I am assuming here that you are using nominal 1" dressed lumber; for other sizes, use a chisel equal to the thickness of your wood.

This drawing shows you how the chisel acts in the operations described—to the left under the heading **Cutting the slots.**

See note **Chisel size** on the opposite page.

Marking with a marking gauge

For accurate and consistant lines, use a *marking gauge.* This useful device is not expensive and lasts forever. Basically it's a stick with a point on the side and a sliding stop that is tightened by a screw.

To use the marking gauge, loosen the screw and slide the stop so that the distance between it and the point is the distance you need; tighten the screw and, holding the stop firmly against an edge, push the point along the wood. There is a bit of skill needed to use this tool, but you will soon get the hang of it.

NOTE how the marking gauge is run at a slight angle to the surface it is marking. When you are used to this, try the rolling motion, which helps sometimes. The motion is turning the wrist as though throttling up a motorbike!

Chisel size

Sometimes you may need to cut out a slot that is wider than the chisel that you have. In this case make extra saw cuts to the size of, or narrower than, your chisel

Assemble the dividers.

Nail in the dividers.

CHISELS

Chisels are perhaps the dividing line between the layman and the craftsman. When you start using a chisel for its proper use—*not* prying stuck windows, *not* opening paint cans, *not* in lieu of a screwdriver—you are on your way to being a woodworker. Congratulations!

Chisels are really just a piece of metal, sharp at one end, and a handle for holding it at the other end. Even with such a simple arrangement, there is a vast array of different kinds of chisel and a variety of quality that can be a problem for the beginner.

I have found that one can buy excellent chisels in any hardware store at a relatively inexpensive price. The most common brand names are Marples Blue Chip (my favorite), Stanley, and Sandvic. You will have to trust that the steel is good, but you can try the handle—hold it in the thrusting position and in the stabbing position before deciding. Hold it as though you were playing billiards—use both hands for this move.

Chisels are measured across the width of the blade. They range in ⅛" increments from ¼" to 1½". Some tool companies, such as Lee Valley, sell sets of five Blue Chip chisels in the most usual sizes. They're a bargain!

As with all tools, the *cheapest* are often the most expensive. So be careful; ask someone who knows (nowadays, generally not the store clerk). Get a catalogue from a good tool company; read, mark, learn, and inwardly digest it.

When thinking about buying a chisel, notice the patina of the metal; good chisels look smooth and deep, not like brushed aluminum! Beware of "real" deals such as a boxed set of six chisels for about the price of a single good chisel. Remember, you are buying a chisel—not a box!

You will most likely find chisels called *butt chisels.* They are short stubby little things and are doubtless good steel. They are made to fit easily into a toolbox and are specifically for carpenters to recess hinges into a door frame. They look so cute and useful that I bought one once and found it to be quite unsuitable for the kind of work that I do. It is too short to hold for mortising, or for paring with pleasure, or for sweeping out curves.

None of the woodworkers that I know have matching chisels, unless they happen to like a particular brand. Even then the individual chisels seem different because of their different ages and amounts of use.

This is one of the keys to real woodworking—buying a tool only when you need it, not because you think it will be useful *someday.*

The chisel shown here, with a blue handle, is called a **firmer chisel.** This is the most common chisel and, as most people don't know its name, they just call it a **chisel.** The firmer chisel is an excellent, all-purpose tool that is good for paring, mortising (making square holes), and trimming. It is strong enough to be struck with a mallet or with the side of a hammer. You can use this chisel for all the jobs in this book.

The front of the blade is beveled on each side, but the back is perfectly flat.

Chisels are sharpened with two bevels on the front—the back is absolutely flat. Keep it that way or trouble ensues! **Be warned!**

A **mortise chisel**, shown to the right, is a heavier tool made for cutting mortises. The blade of the mortising chisel is square and thick. Sharpened with a steeper angle, it is a strong tool for the heavy work of cutting into hard woods. Often there is a leather washer between the blade and the handle to absorb blows of a mallet.

The handle generally has **ferrules** to stop splitting from repeated blows to it when mortising.

The mortising chisel does not work well as a general chisel, but for mortising there's nothing to beat its lovely, solid efficiency.

Chisel blades are fixed to the handle in one of two ways. The blade fits into the handle or the handle fits into the blade. The chisel shown here has the handle fitted into the blade; it is a **socket chisel.**

The **mortising chisel** at the bottom of the page has a **tang** on the end of its blade that fits into the handle. If you are buying a new chisel, check that this join is good and has no "wobblies."

Two bevels

Ferrule

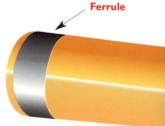

This is a _firmer chisel_.

Because the handle fits into the blade, this is style is called a _socket chisel_.

The back of the chisel is flat.

Old chisels are sometimes dried out and the blade is loose—this can easily be fixed if the handle is wood. Use a little pine resin. See "Your Own Knife" on pages 60–61.

Make sure that the handle is in line properly with the blade and—especially with squarish section, plastic handles—that the surfaces of the handle are lined up properly with the surfaces of the blade—not a big problem, but it can be irritating.

All tools have their little quirks; you come to know them and allow for them after working with them a while.

My friend and cabinetmaker, Henk, says, "Never buy tools from guys who have used them for making a living—they know their little ways and know that if you hold it maybe a bit to the left it'll work the way you want it to!" I've seen him lining up to buy tools from guys who make a living at it, though!

Protect the cutting edge of chisels by putting a piece a blanket or felt under them. Those who like to keep chisels in a roll of canvas or soft leather make sure that the cutting edges don't touch each other when rolled up.

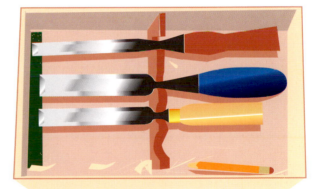

If your chisel assortment starts to look like this, you're in good company.

Ferrule

Leather washer

Blade

ACME MORTISING CHISELS

This is a _mortising chisel_.

The Loon
WEATHERCOCK

Have you ever tried to make a loon's call? It's not as easy to do as it may seem to be.

But when you hear that lovely, plaintive throat warble, it goes right down to your heart. I can't promise that you'll get

the same feeling from this weather vane, but I hope it will remind you of those wide, quiet places where you last heard it.

Loons are often so far away that it is quite a surprise to some people to learn that they are about the same size as a turkey.

They swim lower down in the water than this weathercock, but if we made him that way he wouldn't be as pretty!

As Pablo Picasso said, "Art is the lie that enables us to realize the truth."

Making the loon weathercock

Projects don't get much simpler and easier than this, yet it is as beautiful as it is useful.

Find a piece of flat wood about ¾" thick. Draw the loon onto the board as it appears on this page (photocopy it and paste it onto cardboard to make a template—because maybe you'll want to make more than one). Cut out the loon with a jigsaw, or coping saw, or whatever you have. Drill a ½" hole for the dowel.

Paint it. Great!

"Whoowwaaaaaarrrr . . ."

Mounting

Get a piece of ½" dowel and a piece of ½" copper pipe, an end cap for the pipe, and two brackets to fit the pipe.

Sharpen the end of the dowel as though it were a pencil. Put the loon on the blunt end.

Cut the copper pipe to be just a little shorter than the distance from the bottom of the loon where the dowel comes out and the point of the dowel. Put the cap on the pipe; glue it, or solder it, or crimp it so that it won't come off. Put the dowel in the pipe. Mount the pipe in a suitable place.

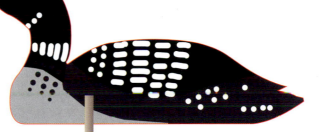

It's enough of a challenge making something nice, let alone changing all these groups of alphabetical symbols (words) into pictures in our heads.

So for those sensible, visual people who like their instructions in pictures—**turn the page!**

Making the Loon Weathercock

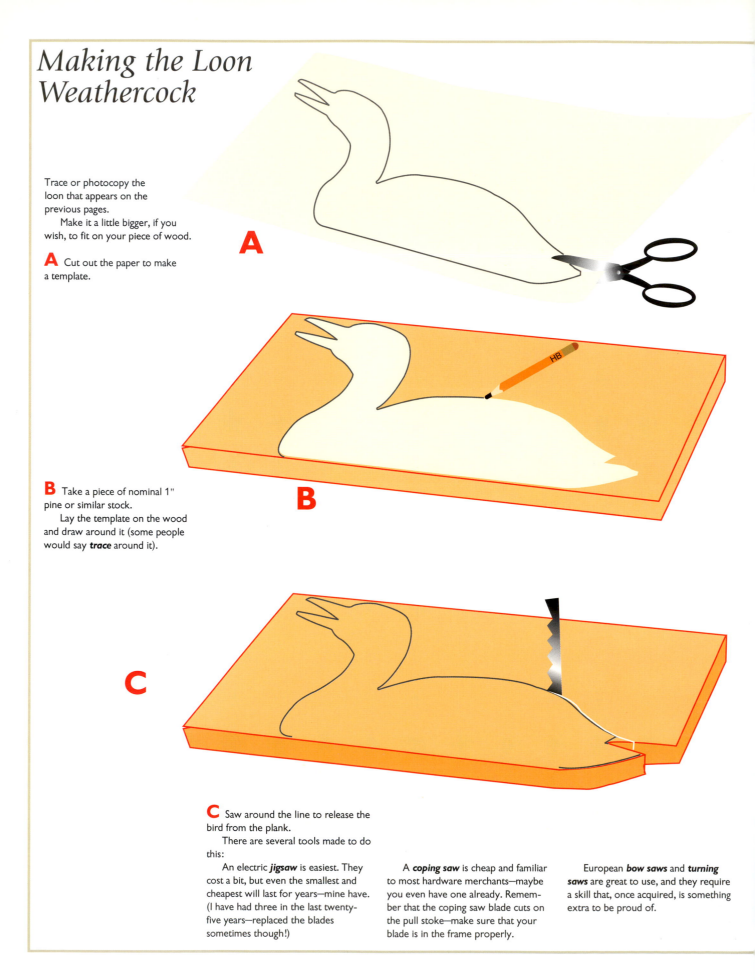

Trace or photocopy the loon that appears on the previous pages.

Make it a little bigger, if you wish, to fit on your piece of wood.

A Cut out the paper to make a template.

A

B Take a piece of nominal 1" pine or similar stock.

Lay the template on the wood and draw around it (some people would say **trace** around it).

B

C

C Saw around the line to release the bird from the plank.

There are several tools made to do this:

An electric **jigsaw** is easiest. They cost a bit, but even the smallest and cheapest will last for years—mine have. (I have had three in the last twenty-five years—replaced the blades sometimes though!)

A **coping saw** is cheap and familiar to most hardware merchants—maybe you even have one already. Remember that the coping saw blade cuts on the pull stoke—make sure that your blade is in the frame properly.

European **bow saws** and **turning saws** are great to use, and they require a skill that, once acquired, is something extra to be proud of.

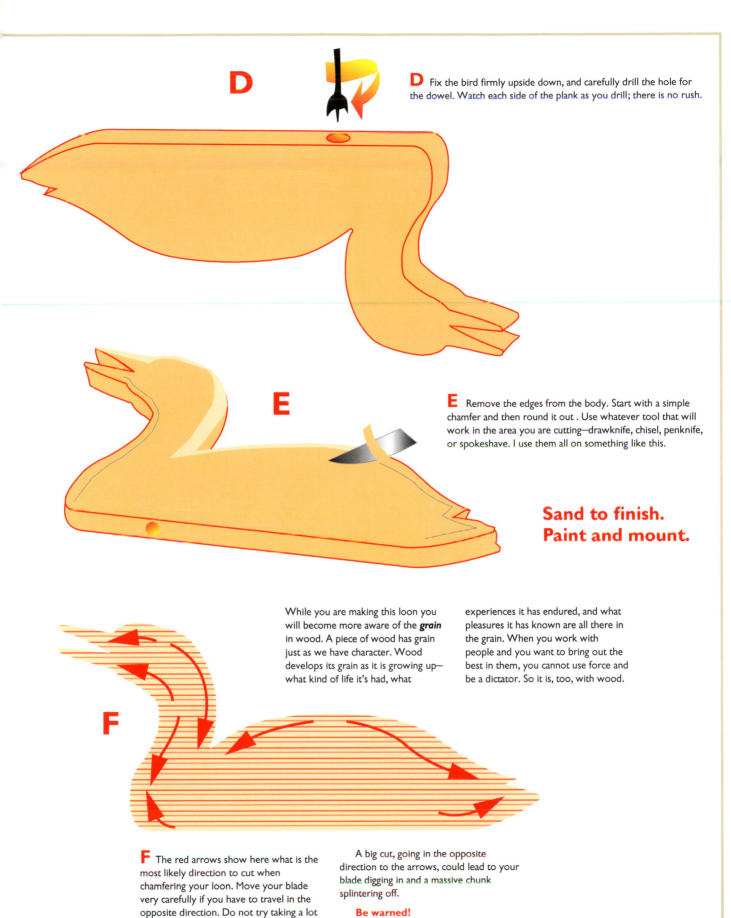

D Fix the bird firmly upside down, and carefully drill the hole for the dowel. Watch each side of the plank as you drill; there is no rush.

E Remove the edges from the body. Start with a simple chamfer and then round it out . Use whatever tool that will work in the area you are cutting—drawknife, chisel, penknife, or spokeshave. I use them all on something like this.

**Sand to finish.
Paint and mount.**

While you are making this loon you will become more aware of the *grain* in wood. A piece of wood has grain just as we have character. Wood develops its grain as it is growing up— what kind of life it's had, what experiences it has endured, and what pleasures it has known are all there in the grain. When you work with people and you want to bring out the best in them, you cannot use force and be a dictator. So it is, too, with wood.

F The red arrows show here what is the most likely direction to cut when chamfering your loon. Move your blade very carefully if you have to travel in the opposite direction. Do not try taking a lot off at first; go tentatively until you are sure.

A big cut, going in the opposite direction to the arrows, could lead to your blade digging in and a massive chunk splintering off.

Be warned!

Nighthawk
WEATHER VANE

N ighthawks are lovely birds and as far as I know cause nobody any trouble. They eat flying pests and look so free, circling above the church spire of a summer's evening.

Making the nighthawk weather vane is just like making the loon weathercock (pages 38–41), but I have added a little flying bug to make him seem even more real.

Making the nighthawk
Find a piece of flat wood about ¾" thick. Draw the nighthawk onto the board as it appears on these pages (photocopy it and paste it onto cardboard to make a template—because maybe you'll want to make more than one). Cut out the nighthawk with a jigsaw, or coping saw, or whatever you have. Drill a ½" hole for the dowel.

Mounting
Get a piece of ½" diameter dowel and a piece of ½" copper pipe, an end cap for the pipe, and two brackets to fit the pipe.

Sharpen the end of the dowel as though it were a pencil. Put the nighthawk on the blunt end.

Cut the copper pipe to be just a little shorter than the distance from the bottom of the nighthawk where the dowel comes out and the point of the dowel. Put the cap on the pipe; glue it, or solder it, or crimp it so that it won't come off. Put the dowel in the pipe.

Mount the copper pipe in a suitable place.

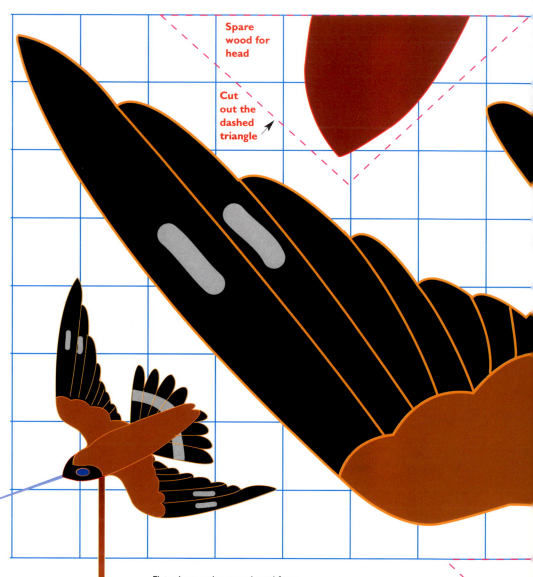

Spare wood for head

Cut out the dashed triangle

Flying bugs make a good meal for a nighthawk. Make a little bug out of a piece of aluminum can—it cuts easily with scissors. Split the end of a chopstick or twig and insert the bug. Wrap a bit of thread around to hold it in. Cut a circle of aluminun and make a tiny windmill. Put the windmill on a pin and stick it in front of the bug.

Drill a hole in the nighthawk's head, and insert the stick—bug an' all.

Attach the dashed triangle from behind the wing area, as shown at the top, and glue it here.

Assembling from pieces
This nighthawk can be made from one piece, but if you are frugal you can saw it from a narrower plank by cutting the head from the spare wood behind its wing.

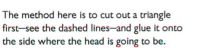

3

2

A

1

The square grid
Sometimes there is
just not enough room
to show an object full size,
and it may not be practical
to use dimensions because
of curves in the work. In such
cases it is common to find a
square grid with or behind the
drawing.

   The squares in this drawing
represent 1" squares.

Using squares to enlarge
(or reduce)
To use the squares, draw a
similar grid full size on a piece
of paper. Pick an area of squares
with something in it—e.g., **A.**
Notice where the image crosses
the gridlines, e.g., about a third
down line **2,** and halfway across
line **3.** Mark those points on the
full-size square.

   To enlarge—if grid is labeled
1" square, make your squares
bigger; e.g., a 2" square will
result in an image twice the size.

   To reduce—make the squares
smaller; e.g., if your squares are
¾" and the original squares are
1", the resulting image will be 75
percent of full size.

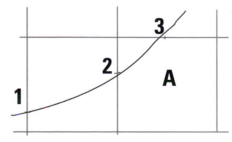

The method here is to cut out a triangle
first—see the dashed lines—and glue it onto
the side where the head is going to be.

   You have a flat area that makes drilling
the hole a lot easier; so drill the hole
before cutting out the bird shape.

When fairing out the line in **A,** don't expect
your points to exactly coincide. You have to
be intelligent and *fake it.*

43

Creating Your Own
WEATHER VANE

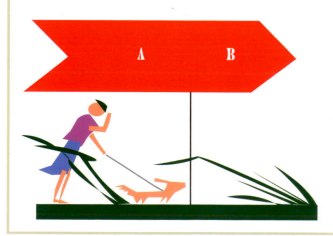

Designing a weathercock

Once we realize that as long as area **A** is greater than area **B,** the vane will point into the wind; then the sky's the limit in weathercock design.

Books on birds and animals are full of drawings that will convert very easily into ideas for weather vanes. Audubon is particularily good, maybe because he drew everything full size but had to fit it onto the page; so the creatures have been "designed" but are realistic. Old engravings of horses and lions and pigs and chickens and boots are *made* for weather vanes.

A hundred years ago people made vanes of the things around them. What do you like—your car, a frying pan, your dog, a friend?

Why weather vanes?

Why are they called weather vanes and not just wind vanes? It's because when you combine the direction of the wind with where it is coming from—and where it *was* coming from— you can get an idea of the changes in the weather and what the weather to come may be.

FROST

One-inch square

A sign or a vane

Here is a sign I made to point the way to a cottage, but it could just as easily be a weather vane. All the pieces are cut out of ¾" particleboard or plywood.

Screw and nail the bits together.

The headband and hair were made from strips I cut from an empty cat food can.

Cut out the letters of your family name and nail them on.

Mount the sign or vane in a suitable place.

BRACE & BIT

A *brace* is a device for holding a piece of sharpened metal and moving that piece of sharpened metal in such a way as to make a round hole.

It is a simple and honest tool that is fast disappearing from the scene. I guess that's because it takes time to drill a hole with a brace and bit—that's what the piece of sharpened metal is called, a *bit*. You will find, though, that you can bore nicer, cleaner, happier and more thoughtful holes with a brace and bit than any that were ever smashed, sawn, or ripped through wood with electricity's★ help!

Using a brace and bit helps in understanding your wood. Listen to the bit as it slices through your wood, feel its tension and release as it passes through the grain. Smell the pine letting forth its bittersweet resin. Cedar, dry and crisp. Spruce, brittle, harsh and worldly.

★ For all my dislike of electric tools, I do concede that the electric drill for small holes is pretty nifty. A hand drill is useful, but expensive, and, since the handle fell off mine, I'm sorry to say that I have been using a small electric drill that I was given as a present years ago. I hear that about 95 percent of homes have an electric drill—maybe your home is one of them.

Auger bits

The three important parts of the front end of the auger bit work together to make the hole. The **lead screw** pulls the bit into the wood; when it is started, the **spurs** scribe and cut the circle that describes the hole. Once the wood fibers having been cut by the spurs, the **cutters** follow along and shave the waste wood away. Chips made by the cutters are pushed up the spiral and out of the hole.

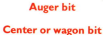

Spurs

Cutters

Lead screw

Auger bit

Size 8 means ⁸⁄₁₆" (½").

Center or wagon bit

Twist bit with square shank

Countersink bit

Technical data

All these brace parts have names. I could look them up if I wanted to know what they were for sure, but right now there is absolutely no point in my doing that.

Bit types

Many kinds and varieties of bit exist for use with the brace. The most common nowadays is the **auger bit.** This bit is measured in sixteenths of an inch. The number of sixteenths is stamped onto the square shank. The example here is a No. 8—so it is ⁸⁄₁₆", or half an inch. At flea markets and garage sales, one can often find the **wagon bit,** a simple but useful tool. If you're lucky, small **twist bits with square shanks** can be found often in old piles of rusty nails and junk!

Bits for electric drills look like those below. The **high-speed bit** is designed for **metal**; it makes a hole in wood, but not well.

The **spade bit** is a forceful thing that at high speed bashes, rapes, and screams its way through wood—used by people who use nails a lot. Metal bits and spade bits present a problem with the traditional brace, because it has a two-jaw chuck; a three-jaw chuck is better to grip the round shanks of these electric-drill bits.

High-speed metal bit

Spade bit

1/2"

 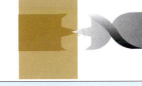 

Using an auger bit
Making a hole with an auger bit is not a matter of just going through the wood and out the other side. If you do this the hole on the other side will be jagged and ugly. There are two ways to avoid an unpleasant exit hole.

Method A
Start the auger screw into the wood and drill until the point emerges from the other side. Back the bit out by turning backwards.

Turn the wood over and drill from the other side using the tiny hole made by the point as the center. A little more pressure is needed here as the lead screw has nothing to pull on.

Method B
Fix a piece of scrap wood firmly to the back of your work and drill right through your work and into the scrap. The scrap stops the splintering as the bit emerges.

Below you see an **ordinary chuck**. Below that, a **ratchet chuck**. Many a brace has this refinement. The ratchet allows you to work in tight spots where a full sweep of the crank is not possible. I have had to use a ratchet brace maybe **twice** in the last twenty years.

Putting in the bit
Hold the brace in the horizontal position, one hand on the crank and one hand gripping the chuck. Press the knob against your body. Swing the crank in a counterclockwise motion while holding the chuck firmly. This will unscrew the chuck a little, releasing the jaws, making room for the bit to be placed in. To tighten the chuck, hold the chuck and swing the crank clockwise. The square shank of the bit must fit down inside the jaws.

Vertical boring with the brace and bit
Secure your work in an horizontal position. Place the center of the bit on the mark which is the center of the hole-to-be. Line up the knob directly behind the bit so that the bit will travel at a right angle through the wood (for other angles, adjust as needed). Press down on the knob with your other hand and turn the crank.

Horizontal boring with the brace and bit
Secure your work in an upright position. Place the center of the bit on the mark which is the center of the hole-to-be. Line up the knob directly behind the bit so that the bit will travel at a right angle through the wood (for other angles, adjust as needed). Press some convenient part of your body against the knob and turn the crank.

Benches and
SHAVING HORSE

Sometimes even independent people like you and me need some help. We could manage by ourselves, but as my dad always says, "Any damn fool can rough it, Rodney, any damn fool can rough it!"

One of my constant companions is my shaving horse; you don't have to have one, but like all friends it makes life a little easier. Just like friends, too, I can't tell you what is right for you, but I can tell you some of the things to consider and a few examples of what works for me.

A *shaving horse* is a bench with a quick-release vise on it. (A *vise* in woodworking is a clamp fixed to a bench or heavy object that lends you a third hand when you need it.)

When you use the shaving horse, you sit astride it as on a living horse, but your feet think they are driving a car.

When I sit down on my shaving horse, I feel right at home with an old friend—and, more than that, it makes me want to start working at something.

You can move your horse to a different part of the garden or, if you are in an apartment, put it on another part of your balcony when you need a change. Sit in the sun in the springtime, the shade in the summer, and when it rains go into the shed or onto the porch.

One of the nice extras that comes with having a shaving horse is that it not only gives you the bounds of your territory—but it tells others, too.

Introducing the shaving horse

A *shaving horse* is really just a simple bench with a clamp on it to hold wood while you work on it. It is sometimes called a *shingle bench* because cedar shingles were thinned and trimmed on it; it is called a *draw bench* by some people, and others say *schnitzel bank.* They are all more or less the same.

A big chunk of wood holds down your workpiece onto a flat shelf and holds the piece firmly for cutting. The big chunk of wood is held down by

your foot, which uses a foot pedal attached by a stick.

The shaving horse can also be used as a chopping bench, a drilling bench, and whatever else you can find useful to do with it.

On my shaving horse I have put a springy twig to open the clamp when my foot is not on the pedal. You will find it useful too, though descriptions of the shaving horse by other woodworkers often don't include one—maybe they never really used it.

Folding benches

Many of you may already have one of these *handy benches.* They are often on "special" at woodyards and hardware stores. They last for years, well mine has; and if you don't have a lot of room or move around from place to place they are ideal. There are several kinds on the market (for more of my observations on their usefulness, refer to page 106).

The view from the drivers seat

Here is what you'll see when you work on a shaving horse. Sit comfortably and relaxed but ready. Put your foot onto the pedal and try it a few times. Put your hands into position as if you were holding a draw knife and do a few motions. It's almost like paddling a canoe.

When you use a draw knife, someone is bound to say that you will cut yourself going toward your body. **Be alert** and it will not happen. If you are worried that you will damage your body, get a leather bib of some kind or use a spokeshave until you feel confident. Nobody is forcing you to do this work and there is no hurry. Take your time you will succeed.

Points of interest

Workbench—This has a slot in it to correspond with the slot in the sitting bench. Through this slot passes the lever that connects the head with the foot pedal.

A *springy twig* and a piece of string make opening the vise easy every time you lift your foot.

The *pivot* is a twig or piece of metal upon which the lever revolves.

Firm ground—Put your bench on whatever surface you want, but make sure it is sturdy and firm.

Wobbly ground is very annoying and takes concentration away from your work.

There is more about making a shaving horse on pages 50–51.

The clamp (head) is often heavy in North America and Europe, but it can be just a bar like English woodworkers use.

This is the **main bench** upon which you sit. Make it nice and wide, but remember that your feet have to operate the pedal.

Anyone that works outside a lot wears a **hat.** Hats not only keep the sun out of your face; they are also a protection against knocks. It may be hard to believe that one layer of cloth can do much to protect your head, but try walking into the end of a plank at the woodyard with and then without a hat.

Wear something **comfortable.** Nothing tight or constricting. Woodworking is not dirty work, but one does get sweaty.

Working outdoors brings one back to the rhythm of variable weather. Rain and snow will fall, so when you get back to work the bench may be damp. If this bugs you, get a cloth or piece of leather to sit on. Remember to take it in when finished.

Lever—Most books will tell you to make this very thick, but I figure that it is for doing really heavy work. For the most recent shaving horse that I built, I used a piece of clear 1 × 4 pine. Works fine for what we need.

Fix the **foot pedal** to the **lever** with a bolt; that way you can take it off if you need to.

Shavings are biodegradable; it pays to remember this when fielding comments. Scoop up as many as you can after working. I like the way the shavings pile up around my body and feet. Smells nice, too.

Footwear is up to you. If your footwear doesn't work too well with your shaving horse, change it—the footwear, that is.

Making a Shaving Horse

Dimensions of shaving horses vary from person to person and from place to place and according to what materials are available. This one is designed to be made from store-bought lumber, such as cedar or spruce. Make yours of whatever you can get your hands on. My latest is made from a discarded breakfast table!

Nominal two-inch lumber will do just fine. Three-inch for the legs, or use 2 × 4s.

The **head** is made from three pieces screwed or bolted together as shown.

NOTE how the **back legs** are taller than the **front;** this makes it more comfortable to sit on.

Don't worry about their meeting the ground at a right angle; just fix them to the bench at 90°.

To get the **height** of the workbench, sit on the bench and line it up with your elbow. Push the **bench support** in or out to get the angle. And if later you find its not quite right, you can change it.

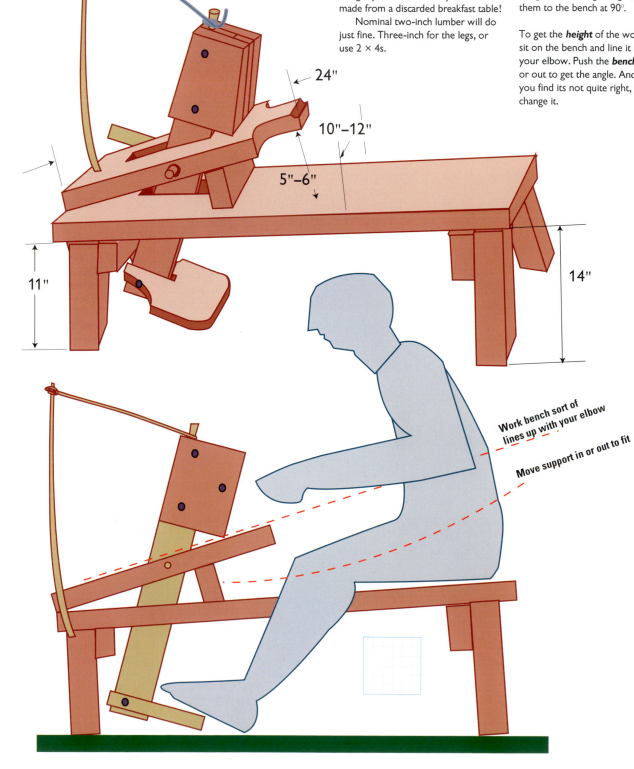

24"

10"–12"

5"–6"

11"

14"

Work bench sort of lines up with your elbow

Move support in or out to fit

50

Customize your shaving horse

Modify the **workbench sides** as shown here, if you want to.

I find it easier to use the drawknife on the side of a piece; so I cut out those two **scoops** on the side.

The **notch** in the end is for propping work between your chest and the horse when using a **breast bib.** Saw this notch to the size you think will work. If it looks like you are making so many attempts that you are running out of wood, screw a piece of wood under the workbench to make a little **sticking-out shelf.**

The **shaving horse** becomes the center of your activities.

Use the jaws for cutting.

Breast bibs work well with the horse.

Push wood against the support as a bench stop for sawing.

Use the bench part that you sit on as a chopping block.

Sit and watch the sunset, or something else, while drinking tea. Have a friend join you or be alone with your thoughts. Pack up, go indoors. Go to bed, sleep well.

Nail, bolt, or screw everything together.

A Useful
STRIKER

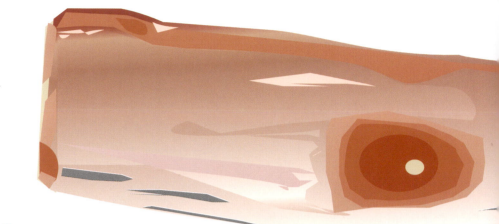

*T*reen is the name given to objects that are discernably made from pieces of tree. Antique stores often have pieces of treen at reasonable prices.

You are not alone

People have always needed useful tools such as this striker that I use when I need to whack a chisel or peg. Make your own.

Treenail (trunnel)

Buggy spokes are not round, nor are hammer handles. When a wheelwright is making a buggy wheel, he does it with the hub upright on the bench, the front of the wheel facing down. The spokes are driven in one on one side, one on the other—gradually crisscrossing the hub, making a cross, then a union jack, then a flower, and finally a starburst.

While doing all this the wheelwright has to fit the tenons snug into the hub, make sure the spokes are lined up with each other, and consider the dish the wheel needs. By eye and by ear the spokes are driven home with firm but sensitive blows. His hand reaches for another spoke in the pile that he has selected.

Picking one up, he jiggles it in his hand while he rotates the hub, bringing the empty mortise to the fore. His hand has felt the egg-shaped spoke and now, as the tenon clicks between the flanges, his ears move wood against metal and the vibration congeals as the spokes becomes as close as if they had grown together into a wheel.

We have a potato masher that is very much like this *striker.*

This *cupboard* or *gate handle* is made from a piece of branch.

Turn it up the other way, and it's a mug or coat hook.

One fixing screw is all that's needed—the other end is held from rotating by a peg known as a *treenail* (or *trunnel*).

Exact symmetry is a recent invention.
Don't worry about exact symmetry.

Sources of found wood

When you are outside—working or not—listen. If you hear a chainsaw, find out where the sound is coming from. Probably some arborphobe has finally had enough . . .

Other people's yard waste

In our area we have days when yard waste is collected—neat bundles of stuff appear at curbside. Just make sure you get there before the collection truck.

Leave it as you found it

Most of this curbside material has been cut into uniform lengths and bundled, usually with very weak string. Make sure that if you get into a bundle it is still tied up when you leave!

Be prepared

Having a pocketknife is handy when on these foraging forays. A pocketful of string may be useful, just in case . . .

Go over and cadge what you need.

If you live near a lake or the ocean, look out for **driftwood.** Both flotsam and jetsam are good sources, often of exotic woods.

Making a striker

Find a log or branch. Green is easier to work. Saw off a piece that feels good in your hand. Work on the wood to make it feel even better for use as a **striker,** driver, mallet persuader, billy—call it what you will.

Use any knife or tool that you feel will do the job of peeling and shaping to fit the striker handle to your very own hand.

What is the wood like?

Under the bark, is it green? What does it smell like?

Look at the rings on the end: are they even, are they close together or far apart? Is there a pithy center?

What happens to the grain when a twig grows out from the branch?

Try the striker out as you go—how does it sound when you whack a chisel or hit a peg?

The shape of my handle

The handle part fits into my hand the way I like. Make yours to be this comfortable for you.

Knife handles are strong and elegant when made from a branch. Visualize the handle in the wood cut away as little as you have to.

HATCHET & AXE

Most often you will find a hatchet in someone's woodshed where it is under-employed and abused as a mere kindling splitter. The handle will be loose and maybe fixed to the head with nails or wire; the head will be rusty, the poll broken and damaged. The edge will be blunt, nicked, and even bent over from hitting the stone floor. It looks bad, but—we can fix it!

Old hatchets are hard to find just as old garbage cans are hard to find; often they are not put in garage or lawn sales because nobody thinks that they are worth anything or they are still using them. Keep your eyes open in the dim recesses of your friends' sheds, outbuildings, and garages. A rusty old hatchet does not stand out for anyone to see, and you have to be a prospector and know where to look.

When you do find one, the best thing to do is to offer to trade a new little axe for it. You can offer money, but if your friend is using it for splitting kind-ling, then what good is money to replace it? If you are very foolish, offer some significant sum; this might do the trick. If at first you don't succeed, etc.; so next time ask again, because people and hatchets are hard to part. A couple of years ago I finally got a beautiful *broad hatchet*. One

Sunday morning a fellow set up his pickup truck in the parking lot at the end of our street and offered for sale the most disheveled group of rusty implements that I had ever seen. For very little I got two garden forks, a spade, a hammer handle that broke soon after, and a wonderful chunk of rust, latex paint, and mud—the broad hatchet! Three hours of cleaning later, I was putting a keen edge on my beautiful "new" hatchet.

One can buy a hatchet through the usual channels, where they often go by the name of *bench axe*. I have seen them in catalogues, and you can get them in real hardware stores. If they are not on display, ask; the clerk will order one for you and be glad to help. I have noticed that often these hatchets are beveled the opposite side to the one that I prefer; so ask about this if you are buying one new. If you are saving one from a fate worse than death, then you will find it easier to make changes to suit your way of working.

People are more amazed at the skillful use of the hatchet than they are about any other tool, unless of course it's the close relation—the axe. Somewhere along the road these two precision instruments became thought of as primitive bludgeons and not as fine shaping tools at all.

No matter what tool you use, the efficiency of the tool depends upon the skill of the operator. This is true from pocketknives to computers. Part of the efficiency of the operator (you) depends on how well you know what a tool can do and what it can't. And even though your tools can do some things, that doesn't mean it's a good idea to do them. For example, a race-horse will pull a plough just as axes will drive steel wedges, but ruin ensues.

To work well, the hatchet must be in good shape. The cutting edge must be sharp, the handle must be firm and

Different hatchets

The definition for a **hatchet**—"short-handled axe"—leaves lots of room for variety in hatchet shapes.

Here are some . . .

They all work for what we need, though I must say that having tried out the kind with a leather disc handle—the **camp hatchet**—I really cannot recommend it.

Blades on which the **cutting edge** is almost **straight** are good.

Axs with **long handles** are fine to use.

Axs that are **2–3 pounds** are good; just hold the handle close to the head.

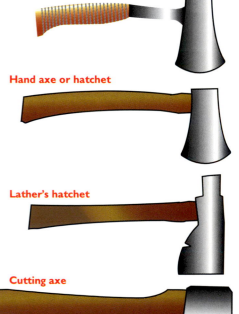

Camp axe or hatchet

Hand axe or hatchet

Lather's hatchet

Cutting axe

secure. The whole hatchet should be clean; no junk, paint, resin, mud, rust, or anything that doesn't belong there. If your hatchet's handle has any varnish on it—take it off. Varnish on a handle makes the handle hard to hold properly. Scrape it off , sand it off, or paint-strip it off—but get it off! Varnish on handles serves only to make them shiny and easier to sell. Human beings are generally attracted by shining objects. Vendors know this and now

Fixing the head to the handle

Don't use metal wedges! The logic behind metal wedges is that they must be stronger than wood so they will work better. This is just not true! Don't cross-wedge with metal; birch bark holds wedges in.

Do this Split a wedge out of some hard wood and trim it smooth—the wedge should be the full width of, and longer than, the slot in the handle. Make sure that the thickness of the wedge at the wide end is sufficient to fill the eye in the head of the tool.

Get some paper-thin birch bark from the outside of the tree. Fold three or four layers of it over the thin end of the wedge. Insert and drive the wedge. Clean down the spare.

Hold your hatchet or axe with your thumb on top. For more control, such as when doing fine cuts, hold it closer to the head.

Broad hatchet handle

The handle of a **broad hatchet** is not straight like a regular hatchet or axe handle; it is curved out to the side. This gives room for your fingers when working close to the side of a piece of wood and enables you to see the work a little easier.

Always check the head of a tool before using. If it is a bit loose, fix it by re-wedging. Do not use tools with loose heads!

This is YOUR responsibility.

Broad hatchet blade

Broad hatchets have a flat side and a beveled side—rather like the chisel and the drawknife. When sharpening, make sure that you don't round out the back—the flat side.

A conventionally sharpened axe works very well for all the work in this book, but keep it sharp!

A Natural
MALLET

Driving stakes into the ground for tomatoes or for keeping idle walkers from the freshly seeded lawn is something that is often done with whatever seems to be handily close by—an chore that can turn into a frustrating experience. The brick that breaks at first blow, the stick that just bounces back, the hammer that, even after you've gone all the way back to the house for it, really is a bit too small!

A garden mallet makes this process so easy. Made entirely of wood found in just about any backyard or wood pile, it will pay for itself in less time than it takes to tell—and it's all yours!

Mallet names

Persuader
Driver
Masher

Though these names all reflect the qualities and purpose of this useful tool, giving tools names can be somewhat of a problem if you do it unilaterally and then have to work with someone else.

Names for things often get in the way of seeing them for what they really are. I once worked for a glass bottle company. We had a stock catalogue of plain jars, each one of which had a name related to the sort of product it might be used for, like *Medium Pickle Jar,* or *Large Jam Jar;* this didn't present much of a problem because there was nothing actually on the jar to say what it was listed as. One day we nearly got a really big order for jars to hold and market samples of a new kind of coffee. The jar that would have been the best for the coffee, in fact, looked as though it was designed especially for the job, but was called—most unfortunately—a *Petrolatum Jar!*

A strange case of tool naming came my way when I was working for wages a few years ago. The shop owner had names for all his tools such as *Bill, Percy, Paul, etc.,* bearing no relation to anything functional! Then in his mid-thirties, he said that all tools must have names because when he was a boy that's what his dad told him. As you can imagine, there were other strange things floating around that

shop, and after two years of going straight I struck out on my own again.

Be careful of naming tools or anything if it comes to that!

Making a mallet

The simplest of all **mallets** is just a slim log of wood. Go find a piece that feels good and hefty in the hand—likely about 3" in diameter and a foot long.

To put a little work into it, shave off a handle part with a hatchet, drawknife, penknife, or all three. The advantage of slimming down the end in this way is two-fold: (1) it's a little easier to hold, and (2) because you have made a handle you are not limited to the size of the log that you can get your hand around. You can use a larger log and hence a heavier mallet.

If all this is familiar to you, it's because you've experienced all this before when making the **striker,** on pages 52–53. If you would like a mallet that is more complicated but just as efficient as the striker, then this one, with a separate head, is only a little more involved, and it looks as though you made it intentionally—not just picked it up off the ground!

Take a piece of tree about 4" across, and cut off a piece that's about as long as the width of your outstretched hand (a span). This is the **mallet head.** Now find a nice sturdy piece of tree for the **handle.**

Use you own judgement as to how thick and how long it must be.

If the wood has bark on it, use a knife of some kind to skin it. In the middle of the head piece, drill a hole to receive the handle. Whittle down the handle at one end, and fit it in the hole so that it passes right through the head and protrudes a bit (the width of your little finger).

Mark the handle on the spot where it enters the head, and remove the handle from the head.

Cut with a saw from the protruding end down almost to the line.

Make a **wedge** that is a little smaller than the diameter of the hole and a little longer than the saw cut in the handle.

Put the handle into the head with the saw cut going across the hole—not end to end! Put in the wedge, and whack it home tight!

Smooth off the end of the handle and wedge. Drill a hole for a string to hang it up.

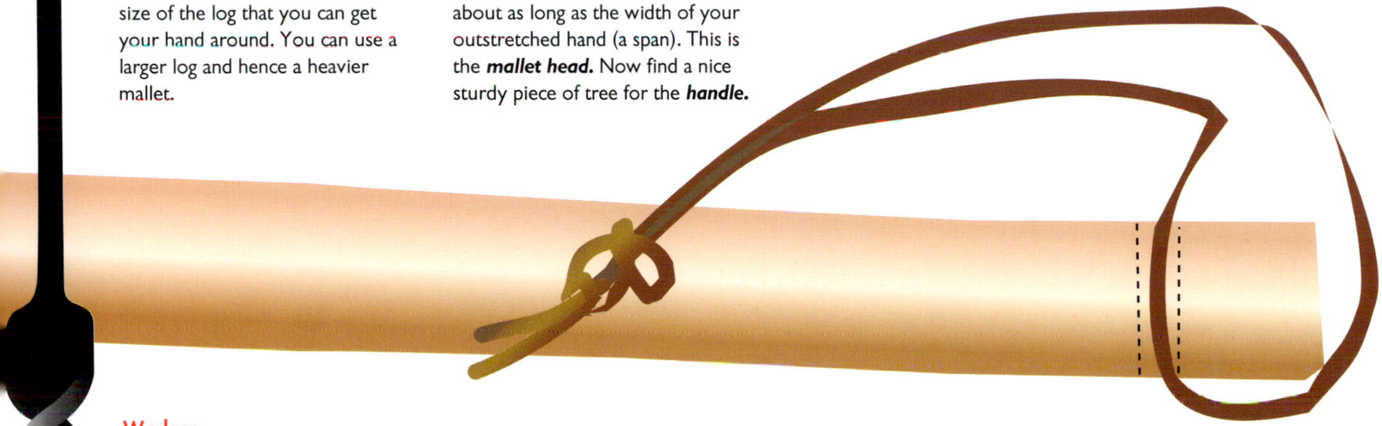

Wedges

Simple as they may seem, **wedges** are something that it's a good idea to pay attention to in the making of (advice that I could use myself). The tendency is to just do something quick, and then you have to fix it up later. If we have enough time to fix it up later, how come we didn't have time to do it right in the first place?

Make your wedges out of some wood that is a bit harder than other pieces. To find out if it's harder, try it.

The question of whether to **saw** wedges or **shape** them with a knife or axe still rages—well, maybe not as much as it used to. How you decide to make your wedges, again, is really up to you.

Here's what I think . . . Split off a bit of wood the

width and thickness of the wedge you need. Chop or whittle it to have a nice taper—not too steep—and then saw it off. Take care that the thin end of the wedge is not too thin or it will break off as you are cutting it. Make the wedge as long as you can; this is complicated to explain—just remember that short, stubby wedges don't hold even with the birch bark to help them. Oh yes—the **birch bark:** take a few slivers of paper-thin bark from the outside of a birch tree, and wrap it onto the thin end of the wedge before driving. This helps to hold the wedge in. I've shown the birch bark on the section on the left-hand page. It is not shown in the diagram to the immediate left for simplicity's sake.

Keep bits of wood around just for making wedges; often a piece of firewood that has been split and ready to go on the fire will have the qualities that you need—riven, straight, dry, clear, and **free** of charge.

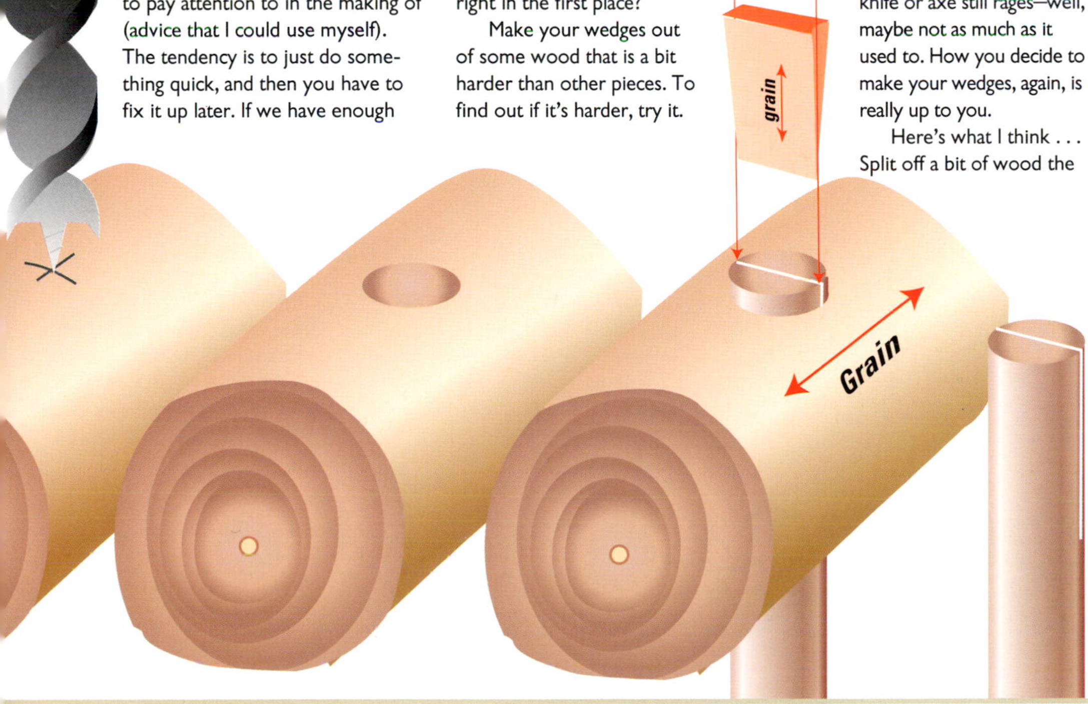

grain

Grain

DRAWKNIFE

One time you could have your pick of hand tools very much the way that you can now buy a TV. Nowadays, saws are easy to find but the drawknife has become scarce.

Real hardware stores in rural areas often carry one or two. They are used for pole or fence post skinning—taking off the bark of a tree. They don't cost much and they last for a very long time. I bought mine 25 years ago and it is in great shape. Even with constant sharpening it should be at least another 75 years before I'm even halfway through the blade.

Because they last a long time, they can often be found at yard sales, tool sales, and auctions. Here the main problem is to out-bid someone who wants to paint it black and hang it in their recreation room! Generally though, drawknives look fairly plain and people drop out when the bidding gets into double figures.

Saving tools to do what they were built to do and not just to be decorations is a constant problem.

Treating a drawknife properly

Do not be afraid of the drawknife. It is big, it is sharp, it is openly big and sharp; but it is like a horse—very gentle if treated properly. And it works so well and so hard that you will ask, "Where have you been all my life?" once you become well acquainted.

The drawknife blade

Drawknives are sharpened like chisels: flat on one side and double-beveled on the other. The flat side is often called the **back** and the beveled, the **front;** however the back is not always the back and the front is not always the front.

Drawknives, like chisels, are used sometimes with the bevel down and sometimes with the flat side down. As a result there are two kinds of cut.

For beginners I recommend the **flat side down** until you are familiar with using the drawknife. Of course, try it both ways; but I find that the flat side down gives a much better idea of the smooth drawing action of the knife, whereas the scooping tendency when the bevel is down is more difficult to control.

When first you use the drawknife, you will be going against all the advice you ever got on cutting things, because most of the time you use the drawknife by pulling it **toward** yourself. **Drawing** it toward you—hence the name.

It is quite safe to do this if you do it properly and heed this advice—**Don't force it!** You could be in a dangerous situation if you do a slicing movement and forget your leg; but even then it will not happen if you are not rushing beyond you capabilities or forcing it—**Don't force it!**

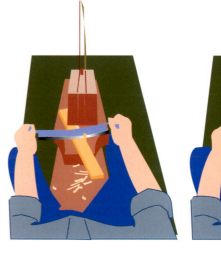

Cutting with a drawknife

There is a strong tendency when learning the drawknife to just put it on the wood and pull. This will work, but it is a clumsy and forceful way to work. Use a gentle slicing stroke.

To do this . . .

Put the bevel up. Extend your arms comfortably. Put the back of the blade flat on the wood. Slide the knife toward you by keeping the blade in contact with the wood, while bending your elbows.

Storage and carrying

Get a piece of thick cloth, canvas, or leather to wrap your drawknife in. This protects the edge from nicks, and will protect anything—arms, legs, fingers, etc.—that is easily damaged!

There is an old saying—

Never cut toward your thumb, always cut toward your chum!

Check out any advice old or otherwise that begins with the word **never.** The advice was coined for idiots and subservient nonthinking underlings, which you are **not!**

There are times when you will need to cut toward yourself with the drawknife—and others when you need to cut away from yourself.

When cutting toward yourself, you have much more control of the tool and the wood and your work.

When you are working with people around you, they often offer free advice on cutting and caution you not to cut yourself. Keep up with your own safe practices, don't get rattled, and after a while the people around you will become more confident.

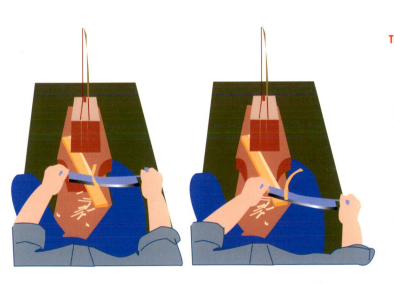

As you do this, move the blade to the side (left or right) so that the blade travels across the wood. It is sometimes difficult to get the blade to cut when first you try this. As you draw back, push down at little, or perhaps you should tilt the blade up a tiny amount. Try it on a rough stick; then try it on some dressed lumber. See how it goes. Nobody's watching—just you.

Trouble shooting your drawknife work

If the drawknife won't slide through the wood and cut in a nice easy way, it could be that:

Solutions

A Your knife is **blunt.**

A **Sharpen** your knife.

B You have taken **too big** a slice.

B Take a **smaller bite** at the wood. I don't mean whispy, see-through shavings, but pieces like from sharpening a pencil.

C The **grain** is twisted or not wanting you to do the cut. (If you wanted to be a rip-snorter of a woodworker, just relax, because in a little while you'll be slicking your way along with skill.)

C Try thin slices, or perhaps you are going **against the grain.** Turn the wood around and try from a different direction. (See notes on **grain** on page 17.)

D You are too **tired** to do it right—this may seem strange to some ears, but it takes a lot of energy to do things and even just to **think**—and there is an awful lot of thinking in making something—ittakes a lot of energy.

D Take a **rest,** relax, get up, walk around, see what's for dinner, go away, never come back—it's your life. Maybe woodworking is not for you; maybe you're right—who knows? Give it another try! I feel just like that sometimes, and I love working with wood.

Your Own
KNIFE

Machine shops can turn out a simple knife in hardly any time at all. A shop teacher told me that once, after I showed him a piece of my cutlery. I still have that knife and I still remember making it and how warm the sun was and how the breeze from the lake bent my unkempt garden.

I hope that you have a nice day or two for making your knife. If a nice day doesn't come at once—be patient—it will, when things are right.

Materials

A mill file from the hardware store or someone's cast-off, worn-out file is all you need for knife-making. Something small is fine, 6" or 8"—perfect.

Tools

You need files and emery cloth. An axe file is all you really need. Axe files have a fine side and a coarse side which, if you know how to draw-file, makes a whole set in one piece. You'll need stones for sharpening, of course.

Draw-filing

To make a deep cut with a file, use it straight. To make a finer cut but with the same side of the file, use it sideways. Fine, smooth cuts are possible with even a coarse file when you use it this way.

De-tempering

Light a **small fire.** You'll have no problem finding shavings and scraps, I'm sure! Put on something more substantial such as small pieces of wood or lump charcoal (not brick-ettes!) to build a solid, healthy fire. If you live in the country, cattle manure that has dried in the sun works very well for this job. Burning "chips" do not smell bad—rather like cigar smoke. (Honestly, and this is no joke, the best cattle manure for this job I have found to be from male animals.)

Putting on the handle

Drill out a piece of wood for the handle. Carve, whittle, and shape it to fit your own hand. The first one that you make may present some problems. It doesn't dawn on you right away, but when it does it is sort of Zen.

Find an abused pine tree and gather some resin from the wounds. Hard, dry resin is good. Crush up a little and put it in the hole in the handle.

Warm the tang—just very warm, not hot. Push the tang into the hole melting the resin. Beautiful smell.

Cool. Sharpen. Use.

Checklist

- De-temper by heating to red heat and cooling slowly.
- Remove teeth from blade.
- Mark blade and tang.
- Shape blade and tang.
- Shape bevel.
- Smooth and polish.

For canoe knife, bend and repolish.

- Heat to bright red.
- Quench.

Metal is now glass-hard.

- Repolish with care.
- Re-temper at 450°F.
- Quench.
- Helve (put on the handle).
- Sharpen.

When the fire has had a good start and has a glowing center, put the file into the middle of it and bring the metal up to red heat. To help retain the heat of the fire, put a piece of sheet metal over the top. Fan some air in. Arrange the coals for maximum effect as you go.

Get the file red-hot all over, then let the fire die down. Do not throw water on it. Let the whole thing, file and all, cool slowly. Overnight is good. If you cannot leave the fire unattended for a long period, bank the fire—put dirt or sand on it and bury it.

This blade is tied on with rawhide. Brass and copper wire can be used.

Drawing the temper

After the first **quenching,** the blade is hard, too hard—it's like glass! When you drop a glass it will generally break, and it's the same with a glass-hard blade—drop it and it will break!

Carefully bring back the shine to the blade. Because the metal is so hard you will have to use emery or carborundum paper. (The wet/dry paper used in autobody shops works well.)

Put the repolished blade on a cookie sheet in the oven. Set the dial for 450°F.

450°F

Come back later and check that the blade has been heated through. This is easy to do because the color will tell you when it's "done."

Remove and quench. Dry off and put on a **handle.**

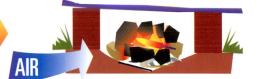

The red heat and the slow cooling render the metal workable by removing the temper.

Shaped handles

Crooked knives need shaped handles to get a good purchase. Find a branch that is almost the shape you need and then make it even more comfortable.

Re-tempering

Light a small fire as before. Get it going well. Put a bucket of water close by—full, not just a dribble. Place the blade in the fire and heat to bright red.

Take the blade out of the fire and drop it into the bucket of water. This is called **quenching.** You might come across a number of ideas about swirling the blade in certain ways and only quenching by magnetic compass points; try them, there's a lot of truth in magic. For now, though, what I'm telling you makes a very satisfactory knife.

Take the blade out of the water. All your polishing is now gone. The blade looks bad, but—we can fix it. Be very careful with the blade; it is **glass-hard** and must have the **temper** drawn before we can use it.

Shaping the blade

From now on, to avoid confusion, I'll be calling the file that you are making into a knife a **blade.**

Remove the blade from the ashes.
File off the teeth.
Mark the shape of the cutting end and the tang (the piece that goes into the handle).
Cut out and shape, using a hacksaw and file.
File on the ground bevel, but leave an edge of about ⅟₁₆"; do not try to sharpen it at this stage even though the temptation is great!
Remove as many file marks as you can by draw-filing and using emery cloth. Get the blade smooth and shiny—it's starting to really look like a knife.
If you intend to make a *canoe knife,* now is the time to put the bend in (see diagrams).
* The blade may seem hard, but it won't hold an edge yet; so we must **re-temper** it.

Canoe knife

After polishing the blade, heat the end to be bent to red heat. Hold the tang end firmly with pliers or tongs. Place the blade over a small log or metal pipe of suitable diameter. Push down on the end with a piece of wood. There'll be a lot of smoke; that's okay, but in all the activity and excitement don't let your hand slip onto the hot metal. Cool slowly. Polish again, and then return to the asterisk symbol * above.

Save the little pieces that are left over—they make wonderful small knives.

The Gardener's
STRINGWINDER

Most people, when it comes to marking out lines in the garden, rely on the famous two-sticks-and-wrap-it-around method—often improvised on the spur of the moment, I'm sorry to say. The resulting piece of equipment works fairly well—once you have unwound the string, and made sure you have the long end, and it doesn't get too high or low, and if the sticks were a just little longer, etc., etc. But this need not be the way. Welcome to *The Gardener's Stringwinder.*

The stringwinder gives gardeners the proper tool to plant and mark gardens that would grace any stately home.

This stringwinder is made of wood that grew in my backyard. Most of it is **lilac;** some is from some other tree that I just don't know. Sometimes it seems like an ash, sometimes an elder—whatever it is, or calls itself, I do know that for small pieces of whitish wood it's very handy.

Lilac is an abundant tree in most areas that have been farmed. Lilacs were planted outside the front door of most farmhouses; so even if where you live is considered downtown, it was pasture not too long ago. Lilac is a hard wood—when dry, very hard—and works to a very smooth finish. In the spring many people seem to use lilacs to express the pent up emotions brought on by the ravages of winter. At this time look out on **yard-waste day** for all the lilac wood you will ever need!

If it's been bundled up, make sure it's that way when you leave.

This stringwinder is made from wood about ¾" thick but, as with all the things in this book, this is not "set in stone."

Stringwinders can be made of anything you want to use; it's the principle that's important. When you make something, it will be many things to you and to other people.

The tree turns into a log, then to a plank, then to lumberyard stock, then to your piece of wood—these pigeonholes are easy to see. But as work proceeds on a project such as this, the wood changes from plank to stringwinder, and there are no easy dividing lines between—only the ones that we make.

Metamorphosis is the underlying structure of the world; it has no beginning and it has no end.

"And to think that a while ago it was just a pile of stuff," said Harold quietly as he stood back to "take in" the popcorn wagon that we had made.

Turn the page for instructions on how to turn wood into stringwinders.

You probably started reading right here in the top left-hand corner. That's what someone who is used to getting information from words does. Those folk who don't have a written language perceive things differently.

Cultural conventions are ingrained in us; they push us around and sometimes make us miss a lot.

Map illustration differs from cartography in that an illustration sort of puts things in the right place; but though it looks like a map, it is not an accurately measured representation. One convention usually applies though—north is at the top of the page. A map I drew of the antarctic landmass had to be revised when three editors (including a yachtsman) rejected it be-

cause they said that I had not put north to the top of the page. (Try drawing a map of Antarctica with north not at the top of the page!)

There is no up or down unless we decide that it is so.

Pictures are a *language.* What do the pictures on this page tell you? Is there a beginning, is there a middle, where is the end? **Why?**

Making a Stringwinder

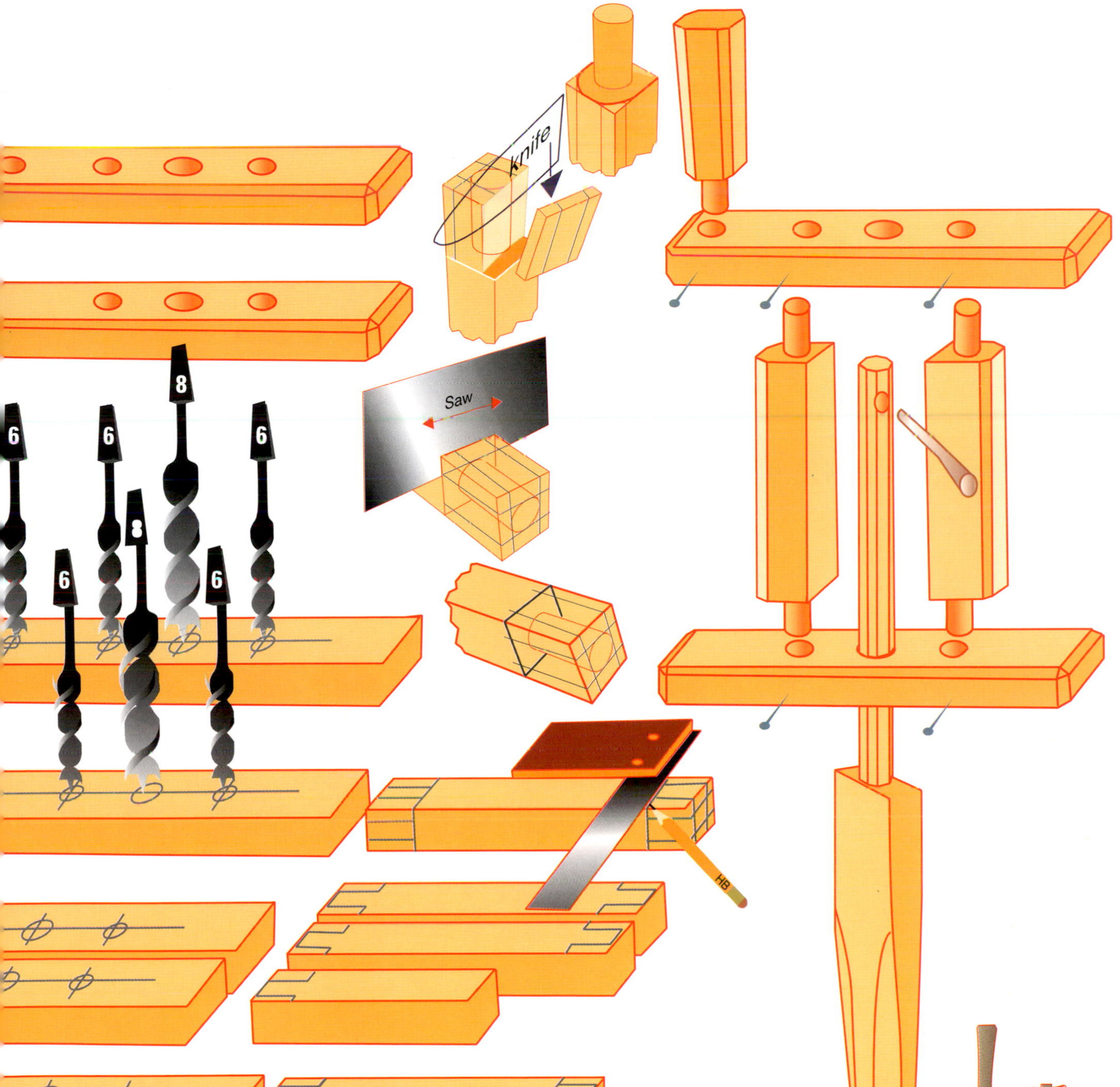

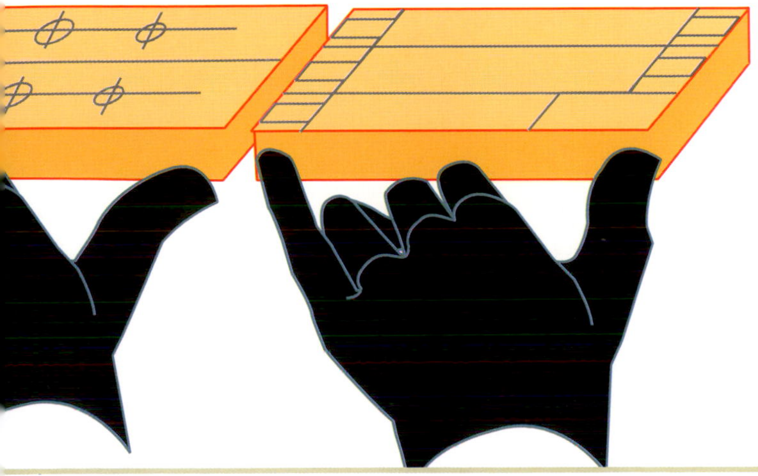

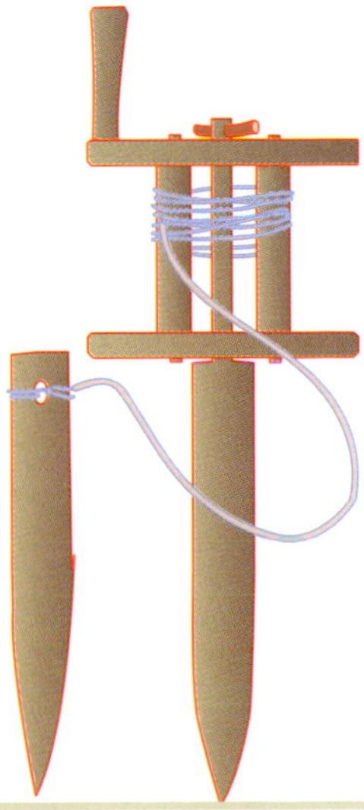

knife

Saw

6 **6** **8** **6**

8

6 **6**

HB

Reading pictures takes as much skill as reading words, but it is not so prestigious in the opinions of those who can only read words; yet to read a thousand words is easier than looking at one picture.

Do not be alarmed at vast and complicated pictures; nobody ever invented a speed-viewing course; take your time.

This page has only two words of explanation—**knife** and **saw**; do not rush, do not try to remember anything—just enjoy!

Bon appetit!

SPOKESHAVES

Potato peeling is a skill that no one thinks of as much of an accomplishment, but it takes a steady hand and eye, exercises the minor motor skills, and requires preplanning strategies and delayed gratification.

When peeling potatoes, if you cut off big slices, each potato gets into the pot faster. But, because the potatoes are smaller from the trimming, it takes more to fill the pot, so that more needs to be prepared; and then one has to work at getting more or making the money to buy some. The truth is, the better you are at peeling potatoes, the less you have to do it.

To help, the vegetable peeler was invented. The idea behind the peeler is consistency—the cut is always the same depth.

By now, when working with wood, you will have found that it is quite difficult to make a smooth and even cut with a knife of whatever kind. Chisels, knives, and axes have a way of wanting to go up and down as well as along a piece of wood when they cut. The cut looks kind of wavy. The spokeshave evolved to help us overcome this and make consistent cuts.

This cross section of the spokeshave cutting wood shows how the *sole* prevents the *blade* from cutting any deeper than it is set.

The spokeshave is a two-handled vegetable peeler for wood.

The **blade** in the spokeshave is fixed to the depth of cut that you need. Spokeshaves exist in various forms but, apart from the sole, of which more later, the only main difference is in **blade adjustment.**

The simplest kind of spokeshave is wooden with a blade that has an upright **tang** at each end. These tangs go into holes in the wood and stick out the other side. To adjust this type of shave, one taps the tang with a small hammer—very tricky to do!

Metal-bodied spokeshaves have two kinds of blade adjustment. The most basic has a **thumb screw** or a **wing nut** on the front that holds the blade firmly. To adjust the blade, you tap the top edge of the blade until the amount that you need protrudes from the sole. This type of spokeshave is the cheapest kind; but beware of cheap tools. The other reason that a good workman never blames his tools is because to a good workman cheap tools are not really tools—they are something someone managed to sell you. Good work can be done with any tool, though; so get what you can afford—that's what I do. The spokeshave that has the two knobs on the top is very finely adjustable. The blade **(cutting iron)** has two slots in the top edge to facilitate two nuts that can move up and down on screw threads. These nuts hold the blade in position so that, when pressure is applied in use, it does not move.

I could not afford to buy this kind of spokeshave. I still haven't bought one—I found one at the town dump. It was rusty, filthy when I took it in. Today it is mature and well behaved, its former life not damaging it in the least, only imbuing it with the fine patina of experience.

Spokeshaves are sometimes called only by their surname—*shave.*

Sole shapes

An important difference in spokeshaves is the **sole contour.** The **flat sole** is good for flat sufaces or convex curves but, because it is flat, it will not fit into concave curves. For concave cutting, a spokeshave with a **rounded sole** is used. The round-soled shave is a bit tricky to cut with, and you will need some practice to make it work with ease.

Why the spokeshave is such a beautiful* tool

* It is easy to use.
* The blade is adjustable.
* The blade can be sharpened.
* It cuts when pushing away from you.
* It cuts when drawing toward you.
* Adjustments are easy.
* It is easy to find and buy from catalogues and stores.
* The spokeshave is not expensive.
* The spokeshave is not large.
* It is not complicated.
* Some are made of wood, others of metal.
* Metal ones are painted in some easy-to-locate color.
* It is quiet.

*In some North American languages the word **beautiful** is the same word as **useful.** Practice substituting them for each other; the effect is revealing!

Adjust the amount the blade sticks out with these.

Here is a typical spokeshave showing all the parts.

This is the **blade.** The bevel is down.

This piece holds the blade firm and serves as a chip breaker.

Knurled nut
—for tightening and loosening the blade when it needs to be removed for sharpening.

The **screw** goes through to the main body part and positions the parts ready for adjustment. In normal use this stays where it is and needs no adjustment.

Sole

ACME
MFG IN CANADA

ACME
MFG IN CANADA

ACME No 15

This is the other side of the blade.

The **bevel** is up.

Spokeshaves come in different shapes and sizes. Some are metal, some are wood. The green spokeshave below is the simple kind. It is cheaper because it doesn't have the fine-adjustment screws, and works just as well. The wood spokeshaves are sometimes found in junk or antique stores.

A Boot
SCRAPER

Even the most efficient tool is not much use if you can't find it. Here's something that not only has it's own marker that helps you find it when it's buried in the snow, mud, straw, or tall weeds, but also gives you something to hang onto so someone doesn't have to come looking for you—in the snow, mud, straw, or tall weeds!

Making the boot scraper
You know, I don't know what I can tell you about making this boot scraper that anyone with their eyes open can't get from looking at the **pictures.**

Get a piece of metal from the tire store or hardware store.

Be careful when drilling the holes—if you're nervous about drilling metal, find someone who isn't. Shade-tree mechanics or the local garage might do it for you for nothing or small change. Better still, plan to make two boot scrapers and give one to the person who drills the holes!

Smoothing uneven wood surfaces
Sawn and split wood pieces often have large areas to smooth away (for example, the sides of the boot scraper uprights, if you've sawn them from a 2 × 4).

A **spokeshave** can handle smoothing, but wouldn't something a little larger be better, perhaps, for leveling the surface? **Planes** are the answer.

A close relation of the spokeshave is the big family of tools that cut to a fixed depth—planes. Not only do they get a bit of weight behind the cutting, but also because of their length it is easier to level wood surfaces with them than with the spokeshave.

There are many books dealing with planes. I recommend that you read some of them.

Nowadays you certainly don't need to know about planes and how to use them until you are quite well advanced in woodworking, because most wood can be obtained already dressed (all the rough saw marks removed).

Paint everything in a bright color so that it shows up in the snow or mud.

Planes straddle the
hills and valleys
when they cut.

Smoothing plane

Made originally to smooth out the furrows made by the jack plane, and shortest of the real planes, this handy tool can give you all the service you need for years. It is a good, less expensive plane for the starting woodworker and the best introduction to the big world of planes.

The short face of the **spokeshave** causes it to follow the undulating surface.

Here are some of the kinds of plane:

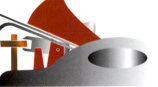

Block plane

This little cutie is often mistakenly bought by beginners because they think that, because they have only a small job to do, this small plane will do it for them.

The **block plane** is often less expensive than **smoothing** or **jack planes,** and this may be an added inducement to purchase; but it is not very useful or as handy as it would appear. The reason is this: Block planes are made with the blade at a very low angle; they are made this way because they are for cutting across the **end grain** of wood. They do not cut off great swaths of side grain. The block plane is made to be held in one hand, and can be useful when you are cutting a long, long chamfer.

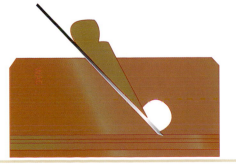

Jack plane

To straighten up a piece or to reduce its thickness, the jack plane is the tool to use. Quite expensive for the amount that you really need it. The picture shows a wooden jack plane; metal ones are more common now, and though I enjoy mature things and old ways I don't see much physical advantage to wooden jack planes.

Molding plane

You will find lots of these in antique and collectible stores. They cut a shape onto the edge of wood and can be handy if you feel frolicsome! Buy a cheap one and try it out. Have fun.

Wood is easily marked. An *ordinary pencil* is fine for the work in this book. A ballpoint pen dents the wood and leaves a sticky ink. Markers have an ink or stain that soaks into wood and will cause trouble later.

Wood can also be marked by cutting or scratching a line in it. The corner of a chisel, an awl, a pocketknife, or even a fingernail can be used. Marking is often called *striking,* hence the "striking knife."

When marking off a measure put a small **dash,** not a dot, accurately in the same direction of the line that you intend to make . . .

In a situation where you don't have a square, use a **book** as a guide to drawing a line.

Using a square

When using a **try** or **combination square,** make sure that the butt is held firmly against the wood.

Put your pencil on the mark, and slide the square up to it. This will allow for the thicknesss of the pencil.

For lines that continue around a piece, notice how much clearance there is between the pencil and square when going across the wood, and apply this distance to the square. Check before striking.

When using a striking knife for this operation, the knife can be held and the arris of the square (where the blade and the butt meet) brought up to it as when making the first mark.

Try square

Combination square

Blade

Stock

Try squares (**squares,** for short) are used to **try** wood, that is, check its straightness and its squareness. **Square** means at 90° to something else. Try squares are used to guide your pencil in making the lines that help you to make square cuts.

A try square consists of a **blade** and a **stock;** sometimes the stock is wood with a brass edge and can run to a bit of money. Combination squares are now common and cheap (in the nicest way). They are very handy and can be used to mark miters, check depths, and scribe lines, as well as many other things.

Try squares are not T squares

even though the name begins with a **T**. If you ask for or order a T square you will get a thing that looks like a T—like this:

Use your finger as a gauge. Good for penciling chamfers. On rough wood beware of splinters.

Marking gauges

A **marking gauge** is basically a stick (stem) with a point (spur) sticking out of the side and something (fence) that slides along the stick to keep a fixed distance between itself and spur.

Marking gauges can be quite simple and relatively inexpensive. **Mortising gauges** could be called **combination gauges** because on one side there is one spur, for single lines and on the other two spurs for marking joints such as a mortise-and-tenon joint. Mortising gauges cost somewhat more than the simple single marking gauge but they are so useful that if you can afford to get one, do. These tools will last forever.

Using the marking gauge

It is simple but does require some skill. Practice on some scraps of wood until you get the rolling motion that you need. Hold the gauge in your hand with your thumb out along the stem and over the fence. Put the fence against the side of your wood and stroke along the wood where you want the mark to be. The spur will make a line in the wood. Sometimes the grain wants to force you astray, so make sure to keep the fence firmly against the side of the wood. There is now on the market a marking gauge that doesn't stray; I tried one and loved it but I think it will be a while before I'll find one in a yard sale!

Close-at-hand measuring

One rarely needs to use a ruler or measuring stick in low-tech woodworking. Learn to rely on your own good judgment when making things. Sure, you're going to be way off sometimes; but after a while you'll get to know where things should be cut and at what angle a thing should be. We all use our other senses every day without question. If we smell smoke, we don't have to look it up in book or measure it to know that smoke means fire. When you eat, you know what will fit into your mouth. If there is a hole in the sidewalk, you know if you

will be able to jump it; nobody, at least I don't think anybody, gets out a tape and checks the distance against their own best record!

At first you will have to use the set standards such as inches or centimeters; but later you will make things to fit human beings or chickens or plants or for whomsoever you are building.

Our bodies can provide all the measures that we need. This has been going on for thousands of years. Some of the measures shown here have names that you will find familiar.

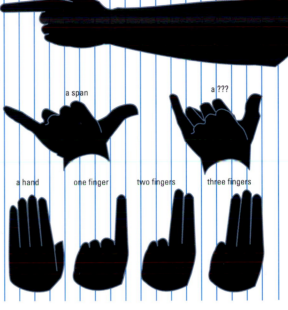

a cubit

a span   a ???

a hand   one finger   two fingers   three fingers

Fingernails and thumbnails mark wood

Use your fingernail and hand as a marking gauge.

If you do not have fingernails—**grow some;** they are inexpensive to keep and are useful for marking, testing the sharpness of tools, and protecting the ends of your fingers.

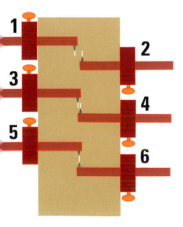

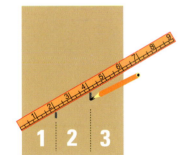

Dividing a board into three

Slope a ruler across the plank so that **zero** and a number easily divisible by three coincide with the edges of the plank. Mark off the three divisions.

Finding the center of a board

Set the marking gauge to the approximate distance between the edge and the center. Test it with a small mark **(1).** Put the gauge on the other edge and mark **(2).** Adjust the gauge to a point between the two marks, and test again **(3 & 4).** Repeat until both marks coincide. This can also be done using a combination square. If you have neither of these tools, then an ordinary stick will suffice.

To find the center of long boards

Take a shorter stick and mark its length from each end of the long board. This will bring the measurement down to something that can be easily managed with a 2- or 3-foot rule.

The folding rule

I prefer this kind. It's called a **blind man's rule** because of the big numbers. These rules are available in folding lengths of 2 feet and 3 feet. They are also made in metric measure if you want to work in that system. These brass-bound boxwood rules can be found in antique stores, junk stores—not so often in yard sales though, perhaps because they always carry fond memories of fathers and grandfathers. They are inexpensive.

Folding rules can be found that have a protractor on the main hinge. On these rules the hinge is a little tighter so that it will hold steady to transfer or draw angles. I once had one with a protractor and a spirit level in it—which was neat and cool—but remember that you want this tool for measuring with; so don't be distracted by extras.

By the way, that long **pocket** on the leg of your overalls is made for a folding rule.

ACME Striking knife

YARD

71

A Peg
BOX

Not until the 18th century did straight lines make a big entry into the life of the common man. Before that we had to rely on the best computer ever to evolve—the human brain. The brain carried around information; it could think in curves and volumes; it could absorb information by being near it; it could process information to the lay of the land, the weather, the human condition.

Three hundred years later we're back with the computer idea, and in the meantime we devised a whole lot of ways of conveying information. Flat.

SCALE 1:1
FULL SIZE

In this **side view** you will see that some of the lines are **dashed** or **broken.** Perhaps you already know what they tell us; about where the hole is or the pieces hidden behind another piece.

In the **front view,** opposite, you will see that some of the colors are **shadowed.** This is just another way to tell you a little about the shape of the box. Our brains and experiences have conditioned us to think in certain ways when we see things like shadows. This is okay for simple shapes, but it's a very complicated way to convey information—particularly as we all have experiences that cannot be the same as anyone else's.

On the next few pages are some of the different ways that people have devised for conveying information graphically, and some ways to relate from one piece of graphic information to another.

This may all seem involved and complicated for "the quiet pleasures of crafting by hand," but it's best to have learned it—and forgotten it. How does that old saying go? **Learn it, forget it, use it!**

Aids to making this nice peg box are presented on the following two pages.

e Cottage Buck Saw Co

Aids to Making the Peg Box

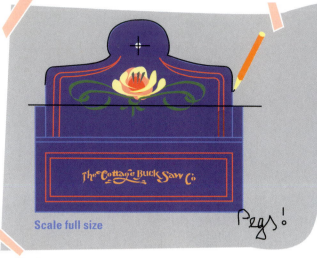

This tool is called a **coping saw**.

It is used to cut curves. You can buy these just about anywhere. They are handy little gadgets and simple to use. The blades fit into the toggles and are held by tiny cross bars. The toggles can rotate to get the frame out of the way. The handle unscrews to facilitate blade changing and rotating. Make sure the blade is tight. The teeth on this saw point down—the cutting stroke is **toward** you.

This diagram is not to scale, which means that the proportions are not the same as for the real saw. It is drawn this way to give you a better picture of the parts.

This is **not a fret saw** those have a finer blade and deeper throat.

ACME COPING SAW CO. CANADA

Scale full size

Pegs!

Transferring

Fix a piece of tracing paper over the drawing that you wish to transfer.

Trace the image and put in a reference line such as a horizontal.

Burrs

As the saw comes out the other side of a cut, it takes splinters of wood with it, leaving a ragged edge. This is a **burr**. Generally we cut with saws that cut going away from us; so the burr is on the back. When using a coping saw or electric jigsaw, cut from the back—if you want a smooth cut on the front.

Use the coping saw *before* assembly

The coping saw is shown here cutting the assembled box **for illustration** space economy **only**. You could do it this way, but it's not very convenient.

Teeth and blades

Once I heard someone describing a difficult task as like pushing a wagon up a hill with a piece of string. String and coping saw blades (which are very narrow) work better when pulled **toward** you.

For a quick check . . .

Gently stroke the teeth with your finger; this will tell you which way the blade will cut. In this diagram you will see that the blade cuts only when moving in the direction of the **green arrows**.

Cutaway views

Getting a good idea of what you are making is sometimes difficult even for the people who do it all the time. **Cutaway views** have been devised to help.

When needed for clarity, the missing parts are shown in broken lines—which does help stop the picture from looking as if a giant rat is on the loose!

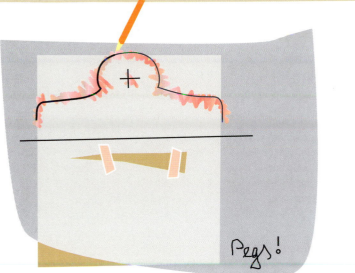

Do not use carbon paper; it stains!

Turn the paper over and rub builder's chalk or soft pencil onto the lines as they show through the paper.

Turn the paper right side out. Place the tracing on the correct place. Draw over the lines with a medium pencil.

The chalk offsets onto the wood.

ONE-INCH SQUARES

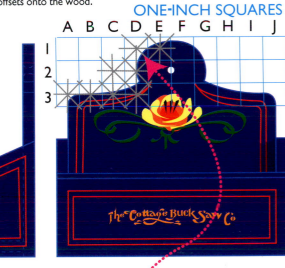

Transferring by squares

An approximation of irregular shapes is possible by using the age-old **square method.** This method requires some skill and intelligence, as it can be frustrating if you think that you are just going to join up the dots for a perfect replica of the image—you're not! Personally, I use this method as little as I can, ever since I gave it a try, at age twelve, attempting to enlarge "St. George and the Dragon"—it was difficult to tell them apart. I've given it several other serious tries since then, but it's not great. I'm telling you this because so often this method is touted as the way to enlarge or reduce drawings, but it's not the be-all and end-all.

point as **square 1D,** the bottom right-hand diagonal a bit more than a third down from the center. That's it! Plot all the others. Sketch in the line. Fix up the line by eye so that it looks right.

My favorite method of enlarging

Eyeball it right from the start; put in the main dimensions and **draw**—this is what you end up doing with the square method anyway. Supplement the eyeballing with a bit of **factoring** (see page 77) and you're all set.

How it's done

Take the picture that has the original squares on it. Draw in the **diagonals.** Draw lines connecting the centers of the squares as now revealed by the diagonals. If they are not already present, write in **letters** for one way and **numbers** for the other—like a graph.

Take a piece of paper and draw the full-size squares onto it . Draw the diagonals. Write in the numbers and letters.

Look at the original and select any one spot where the drawn object crosses a line. In the diagram I have put a highlighted point in magenta; notice how we could describe this

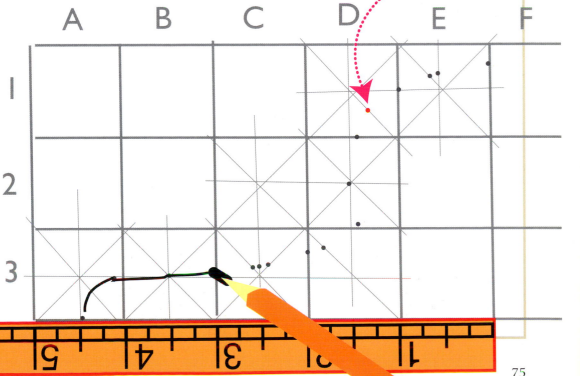

Garden
TOTE

The price of shallow gardening baskets nowadays might have fed a family of sixteen for a year not so long ago. Great for the makers at last to be paid an honest day's wages, etc., but it's ironic that what was once a working tool for peasants now they would not be able to afford. The principle of such developments has so far eluded me; all I know is that one day I needed a box to carry stuff around, and I had a lot of plywood scraps from my sign shop. So I built this handy box to put my things in. It's basic color has the rather chic name of *avocado*.

Such sophistication is not often my wont, but when the general store had a sale of that color, who wants to be considered a yokel?

Making the garden tote

Half-inch plywood is good for this, and a bit of pine or whatever you've got for the handle. Everything that you need to know is here on these pages, *somewhere*.

Notice that the bottom and the ends are the same width. The sides are the length of the two ends and the bottom fixed together. The handle is the same length as the bottom.

Shape the handle from pine, or whatever. Make sure that the ends of the handle are square so that they will fit snug and flush between the ends. Chamfer the middle parts of the handle to make it more comfortable to hold. The handle has two nails at each end; one nail would be sufficient for strength, but the second nail stops the handle from revolving.

The Cottage Buck Saw Co

When you need to remember which is the centerline, mark it like this.

Laying out the ends can be done with a couple of tin cans or something round of suitable size.

1 Measure the height and width of your box onto your plywood.

2 Draw the centerline, and put the smaller can on one end to be drawn around.

3 Draw tangents to the circle down to the bottom corners.

4 Mark the height of the sides across the board.

5 Put the larger can on the board touching the tangent line and the point at the top of the side.

Scale half full size

Changing scale by factoring

Obviously some things are bigger than the page of a book; so to show them, they must be drawn smaller than full size. They are reduced in scale. This scale is noted on the drawing in several ways; sometimes it says, for example, *Scale half full size.* To get the full-size measurement, you measure the drawing with your own scale (rule) and multiply by two. If the scale is one third, then you multiply by three. This number is called *a factor* and this method can help you draw things even from photographs. Books and catalogues generally note a height or width of the object. Let's say the height of a blanket chest is stated as 24 inches. Measure the height of the chest in the picture—for example, 2 inches. Divide the 2 into the 24 to get a *factor* of 12. Now all you do is measure the other parts of the chest and multiply them by this factor to get their full-size dimensions. Of course you have to use a bit of intelligence and allow for perspective, but you'll get close enough to give you a good start!

A Tool
CADDY

Call this a tool caddy if you wish; I just called it that because that's what I use it for—but—remember the *Petrolatum Jar!* (See page 56.)

Making the tool caddy

The difference between this box and the one on the previous pages is that it has a divider in the middle and the sides are shorter. You don't have to have the divider—the box is fine without it—but it does help when you are looking for a particular tool. So do the shorter sides.

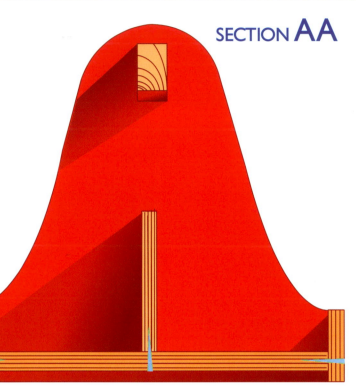

Sections

Above is a **cross section** or **section.** Cross sections are shown to give a view of what is happening inside an object.

A cross section is a slice through an object, and you are told where it is by letters; this one is a slice through **A–A,** seen on the **front elevation** and **plan** views.

Cutting curves with electricity

Jigsaws, saber saws, or whatever the market calls them this year, are pretty handy tools. I have had one for years. Actually I have had three; they do wear out after a while, but you do get good value for the money. One does need an umbilical power cord to the rest of the world, but only briefly. When I am using this tool, I generally go somewhere away from people so as not to annoy them with its noise.

Very little skill is needed to operate this saw, except to **remember not** to put your other hand **under** the board to feel the blade when it's running!

Blades cut on the **upstroke** with a jigsaw; so the underside cut is neater than the top side. If your project needs a smooth cut on the face and not the back, cut from the back, and the front will look nicer.

You will find a variety of blades at the store, from rough cut to very smooth—you decide what you want to use for each project.

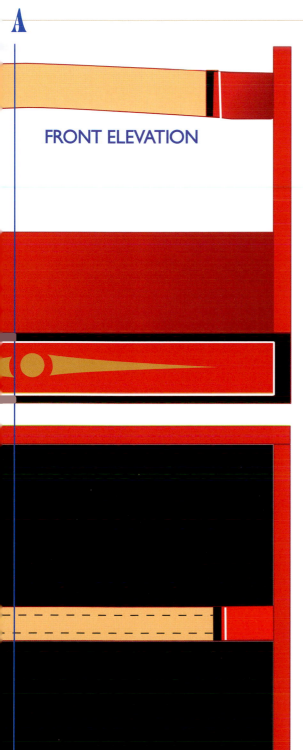

A

FRONT ELEVATION

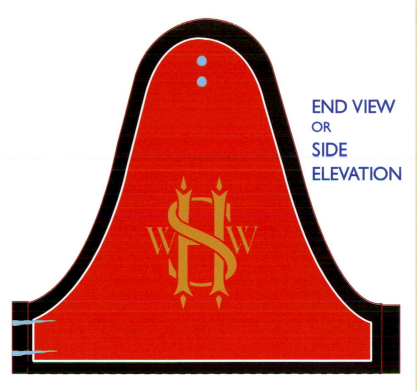

END VIEW
OR
SIDE
ELEVATION

PLAN
VIEW

A

Views

Plans are commonly thought of as any picture of a technical nature. That's okay, but a **plan view** is really just what you see when you look down on an object. The other views are generally called **elevations.**

Painting your caddy

Decorating something is not a willy-nilly activity; it has its basis in culture and perception.

Before we learn to read, we view things differently from the way we view things when we are able to read. Reading teaches us to scan—our eyes run over the page to find out what's coming next.

This is difficult to comprehend until you try this **little experiment:** Take a small cardboard tube, the kind that bathroom tissue is wound on. Put it up to your good eye and look at something in the room—the couch, a wall. Notice how each part is viewed separately by you and when you get to a corner you say to yourself, "Oh, the corner."

Decorating serves to tell us when things are about to happen and to emphasize shape. This is why a threshing machine from a hundred years ago has all its separate parts decorated individually. They do not flow together as we are now used to. Streamlining only happened in the twentieth century, when most people could read.

This box has black edges for a good reason. Years ago, every time one needed paint, it had to be mixed from the necessary ingredients. Matching the same color was a very required a lot of skill. Not only did you need to mix the same color, but you had to mix it to the way it looked now—even the best paint fades and changes according to what's under it! So some brainy person somewhere came up with this solution.

Most damage—dents, scrapes, knocks, dirt—occurs on the edges of things; so paint the edges with a color that is nearly always the same to most people—black. Black is always black! Well . . . close, anyway.

Fixing Up
OLD TOOLS

Beauty is in the eye of the beholder; so I've heard. As I mentioned earlier, in certain languages the word *beautiful* also means *useful*. Another saying tells you "beauty is only skin deep"—maybe we should change that to "ugly is only skin deep." Well, this seems like a pretty strange way to start off a discussion on how to fix up old tools, but then again maybe it's not.

I don't know if I mentioned this before but, hey, I'll say it again: Tony Burlack, who taught me to build and repair wagon wheels, had a favorite saying. Whenever we would heft a decrepit piece of rotting wood and iron on the bench that had once been a gleaming, crisp, efficient and round wheel, he would look at it slowly and then say, "Wellll, it looks bad . . . buuut . . . I think we can fix it!"

So when you find a draw-knife or whatever you've been looking for, give it a good slow look over and wonder if you can fix it. Here's a list of things to look for and a few tips on getting these old tools doing what they do best—nice work.

Reminder
We are not tool collectors!

If a tool is so beat up that it needs an absolutely massive amount of repair to get it into working order—don't bother!

There are people who love fixing up tools for their own sake.

Care for your tools, treat them with respect and understanding, but do not—*do not*—fall in love with them!

Getting off rust
Just about all old tools have rust on them somewhere. Some have a little, some have a lot. In fact, some have so much rust, mixed with manure and paper and string and you name it, that it may be hard to even recognize them as tools at all!

Scrape off bumps and lumps with a paint scraper or a piece of hard wood. At this stage you could even use water to help loosen any garbage stuck to the tool.

Don't worry about the water causing rust, because you'll be drying it off before anything bad can happen.

Squirt some *penetrating oil* onto a small area of rust. Let it soak in.

Take a strip of *emery cloth.* Rub the part that you have oiled. This will make a red–brown mud that may need to be wiped away with a *rag* so that you may be able to see how you're doing. Repeat this over and over again until the tool is as bright as you require.

Working edge
No matter how lovely a tool looks . . . no matter how long you've been looking for it . . . no matter how fancy the decoration . . . no matter how expensive it is . . . if the *cutting edge* is no good, don't buy it! (I'm assuming here that you want it for working with and not hanging on the wall! You're not a collector.)

To know whether the cutting edge is any good requires a bit of research on your part. Go to the library or browse at one of those big bookstores that don't mind if you just look; get some books on tools, any books, all books, and get to know tools. If you're in my area, look me up; I'll help you. If you're not near me, find someone around where you live; they generally love to talk about tools—don't be shy, but, just as when buying wood, don't be pushy.

The *working edge* should be more or less "complete"; that is, it should not be corroded or badly pitted with rust. Sharpening a tool means taking off a *little bit* of the working edge. After a while the hardened edge is worn completely away, exposing the softer body of the blade. This metal corrodes into what sometimes looks like the surface of the moon. The edge will look all wavy and irregular. This is not good!

Pitting from rust will affect the edge; some rust is inevitable, so you decide if it's what you want.

Handles
If water rusts away metal, *wooden handles* can be devastated by it. Wood handles have to withstand the double trouble of water and sunshine. The water soaks in, the sunshine (heat) dries it out. I should say it dries it out and then in, because the outside dries first, shrinking as it does so, while the inside is still damp and swollen. This dry outside is not as flexible as when it was wet, and so it cracks. The next time the handle gets wet these cracks let the water further in, and pretty soon there are bigger cracks and rot. A little while later only bits of the handle remain; then no handle at all!

There is a good side to all this—bargain prices. I guess most people don't know how to put on handles. They are also inclined to consider the tool with no handle just a piece of scrap metal—which of course it is, unless you want to work with it. No problem!

Remember—we are not buying and fixing up these tools to be collectors; we are going to work with them. I could go on telling you of all the possibilities of fixing up this and that, but the amount that you might actually want to fix is related very closely to your situation. Sentimental value, availability, and budget will all contribute to the amount of tool-fixing (restoration) that you do. Some tools have particular problems; these are outlined on the opposite page.

Particular problems: When it comes to fixing up old tools, they're just about all the same; but some tools have particular problems as well.

Drawknife

Rust: See **Getting off rust.**

Missing handle(s): Remove riveting and washer (if still present). Make and fit new handle.

Bent tang: The tang of a tool is not hardened metal and can be bent quite easily. Secure the tang in a vise, and squeeze out the bumps.

Burring on the back (probably caused by someone using a hammer and the drawknife to split wood): file flat to remove upset edge. The back of the knife must be flat.

Saw

Rust: See **Getting off rust.**

Kinks and warps: Take it to a sharpener/expert and ask about it. Straightening blades is pretty tricky. If you really must do it, then get a book, study it, and good luck!

Metal spokeshave

Parts missing: Get a book that has a diagram of the kind that you have and want to improve. Check to see if all the parts are there. Tightening bolt/nuts can be replaced with a bolt that has the same threads; check it very carefully and gently—don't force it. If you are unsure, take it to a garage or machine shop and they will tell you what fits. Adjusting nuts present more of a problem; I don't know who sells these—anyhow these are sort of similar to replacing a spokeshave blade which costs so much that, unless you really must fix the old one up because it belonged to your great uncle's grand-father or something like that, it's cheaper to find one that's in a condition, closer to being ready to work with!

Rust: See **Getting off rust.**

Nicked edge: Re-stone, resharpen.

Chipped paint: Never mind.

Wooden spokeshave

Rust: See **Getting off rust.**

Worn wood: The mouth is often worn away at the back, but this doesn't seem to affect the efficiency of cutting except that the cut is a little deeper. Many wooden spokeshaves are repaired with a metal plate on the back, but I would prefer to make a new handle if the blade is good.

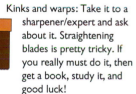

Chisel

Rust: See **Getting off rust.**

Blade loose: Remove blade. Put a little dried resin into the hole. Warm the tang and push it into the hole. The resin melts and fixes the tang. Be careful not to heat the blade too much as the resin will become too hot and not hold. The tang can be held into the flame or on the hot element of a cook stove. Holding the blade in your hand will ensure that you don't use too much heat. This method is good for files and other handheld tools. Get dried resin from a coniferous tree; you will find it where branches have been removed.

Nicked edge: File down and resharpen.

Missing handle: New handles can be bought at most tool shops and suppliers. They may cost more than you paid for the chisel, but you could always make your own handle.

Hatchet and axe

Rust and who-knows-what?: Hatchets and axes get more abuse than anything else; they are found encrusted. Poke, pick, scrub; you won't do as much harm as anyone who had it before. See **Getting off rust.**

Working edge: File back to sound metal. Sharpen.

Handle: The biggest problem is the spot where the handle goes through the head. Check it. The handle should be firmly set in. Weather and ignorance have been the main foes here. Nails and metal pieces are often found to have been used in futile attempts at repair—get them out! Reshape the handle if there is enough sound wood remaining, or get a new handle. Wedge with wood and birch bark.

Brace and bit

Rust. See **Getting off rust.**

There are so many different makes and kinds of brace that one rarely comes across two of the same kind; so cannibalism is out. If a brace is so beat up that it needs special attention other than cleaning and rubbing down with a little oil—don't get involved. They aren't very expensive new.

Box for KNITTING NEEDLES

Visit me sometime, and I'll chatter on about a lot of things that boxes and tools bring to mind; so why should my book be different?

This box was designed and made by me for my wife, Elizabeth, who, when she's not trying to train me to be housebroken, knits up one hell of a storm. Her many needles were in a mess, the cloth roll she kept them in, ragged. This Christmas I thought I'd make her a box. Partway along, just as the snow had started to fly, I said, "Well, you'll never guess what I'm making you for Christmas," and she said, "A knitting-needle box?"

I don't know what the moral of this tale is or even if it has one, but that's what I think of when I see this box.

Saving space is the reason for producing one view on top of another. An elevation is put on top of another elevation in some spot where nothing much is going on. Benches, chests, boxes, and anything that has long parts like this knitting needle box are subject to this treatment.

Printing drawings small is another way of saving space and, because it would be difficult to put in all the dimensions clearly, a scale is drawn for you to step off from. Stepping off can be done with a bit of paper and a pencil, but it's better to use a pair of dividers or a pair of compasses with a very sharp pencil in them.

When you are scaling up remember to use your smarts. What happens is that you cannot be totally accurate—but neither is the drawing. A tiny difference in a measurment at the small scale will be magnified by as many times as the **factor** that you are using.

Inches

You will find drawings like this in old magazines and books—and, I'm sorry to say, in a lot of new publications.

I've drawn this one up big to give you an idea of how the mind is supposed to work when it sees such a drawing.

One foot

A Knitting Box for Mother

More on constructing this box is on the following two pages.

Piano hinges

Piano hinges come as long strips of 2 feet, 3 feet, or a meter. Brass, imitation brass, bronze, chrome, and nickel plate are all readily available.

Buy economically, but don't worry about getting too much; you can always use the offcuts. To cut the piano hinge to length, use a hacksaw. If you don't have a hacksaw, don't buy one; they are generally rubbish unless you get a professional one and then, of course, you're into the big bucks—and besides, I'm going to show you how to make a really good little hacksaw, later.

Countersinking

The screw holes in hinges are not just straight, they're bigger at the front than at the back. Examination will reveal that the hole is actually part of a cone. This is called a **countersunk hole.**

Screws fit into this countersinking and so don't stick out above the surface. When buying screws, make sure that they are not too big for the countersinking in your hardware.

Hinges

Hinges are fun. I love to just stand there with a hinge and wiggle it back and forth, don't you?

Hinges are made of just about any material that ever existed. Wood hinges are nice. A piece of leather nailed on works well. Hinges have wonderful names for their parts like **gudgeons** and **pintles.** A trip to the "supermarket woodyard" will reveal all kinds of new inventions that are nowadays' hinges. For us the old-style butt, strap, and piano hinges are all we need.

Butt hinge with removeable pin

These are very handy to use because you can just pop the pin and do work without unscrewing everything—an activity that leads to looser screws the more times you do it!

Butt hinge

T hinge

Strap hinge

Hinges come in all shapes and sizes.

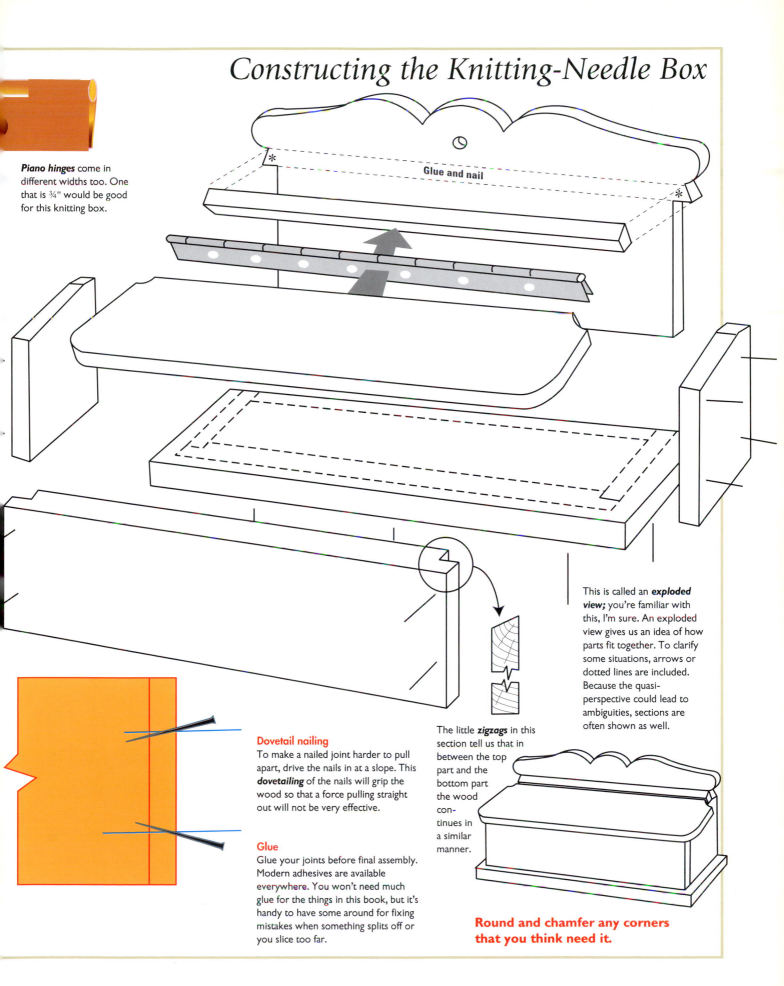

Piano hinges come in different widths too. One that is ¾" would be good for this knitting box.

Glue and nail

Dovetail nailing

To make a nailed joint harder to pull apart, drive the nails in at a slope. This **dovetailing** of the nails will grip the wood so that a force pulling straight out will not be very effective.

Glue

Glue your joints before final assembly. Modern adhesives are available everywhere. You won't need much glue for the things in this book, but it's handy to have some around for fixing mistakes when something splits off or you slice too far.

The little **zigzags** in this section tell us that in between the top part and the bottom part the wood continues in a similar manner.

This is called an **exploded view;** you're familiar with this, I'm sure. An exploded view gives us an idea of how parts fit together. To clarify some situations, arrows or dotted lines are included. Because the quasi-perspective could lead to ambiguities, sections are often shown as well.

Round and chamfer any corners that you think need it.

Even though the old saying, "Putty and paint will turn the devil into a saint," is true, it really helps if your devil has been well cared for during its growing stages.

Finishing starts at the beginning. So don't be doing goofy stuff and thinking that the paint will cover it up. Maybe it will to a certain extent, but, really, you're not fooling anybody but yourself.

Many people have a great liking for the look of wood furniture just plain. Pine looks like pine, oak like oak; sometimes this is nice, but too much is more than a feast. Some years ago there was an outbreak of the dreaded "stripping fever" and there wasn't a town or village that didn't have a shop where all the lovely painting on furniture was lost forever. Because of this most folks don't even know now that furniture was painted in the old days.

Why, I am sometimes asked, did those old guys paint over such lovely wood? What they wanted was something colorful, something that looked expensive. Many of the styles that we have today came by way of imitations—of carving, brass inlaying, and veneering with exotic woods.

Decorating is done because of people's different perceptions. Before we learn to read, our eyes

observe each part. Scanning is one of the reading skills; it helps us to know what is coming next and be ready. Try looking at something through a paper tube, as I suggested in the little experiment on page 79 under "Painting your caddy." This is why edges were marked with stripes and lines, centers of panels defined, arrises given extra highlights, and corners given mind mazes of flowers and leaves like the corner of a beautiful garden.

I love painted furniture; it's an adventure into someone else's tactile mind. What do you like?

Various types of paint

The **solvent** is the main difference. This is called the **base** as in oil-based paints, water-based paints, and so on.

There are advantages and disadvantages to all types of paints.

Water-based paints

Latex, emulsion, and acrylic paints all can be thinned with water. Unfortunately, water affects wood; it soaks in and makes it swell. When it dries, most of the wood returns to it's former size, but lots of fibers still remain standing up. Even very, very well-smoothed wood will do this—it's called **grain raising.** To try to sneak up behind it and beat it at it's own game, what you do is wet the grain with plain water, let it dry, and then sand it smooth again before painting. Then when you paint, it doesn't raise the grain so much.

Acrylic paints are a recent invention and work quite well. I haven't given any an outdoor test, so I don't know how they weather. Craft stores now sell little bottles of paint with folksy-sounding names; they work really well and come in a vast array of colors. Artists' paints are good for decorating and mixing.

Oil-based paints

Turpentines and paint thinner are used to clean this paint off your brushes, clothes, and wherever. If oil paint needs thinning, it's probably "gone off." The technical name and reason escapes me at the moment, but it's enough to know that **if the paint is a gooey mess, it ain't no good.** So, don't use it!

Oil-based paints are made of oils, turpentines, driers, pigments (which give it the color), and other stuff. The pigment in common **housepaints** is added in just the right amount to have the paint look a particular color. Sign paints, though, have lots of pigment. They are called **lettering** or **bulletin enamels.** They are expensive and you need to have a bit of skill in using them, but it's better to put on two thin coats of bulletin enamel than four or five of cheap paint.

Oil-based paints are the traditional **outdoor paints.**

Shellac

Believe it or not, shellac is made from bugs that eat trees in India. **Lac beetles** exude a sticky substance that is made into shellac.

The solvent for shellac varies in name according to where you live. It can be called methylated spirits in England, denatured alchohol in the United States, or methyl hydrate in Canada.

Knots have a way of discoloring any paint that is put over them; so, before any painting, give them a couple of coats of full-strength shellac to seal in the knot juices.

Wood is an absorbent material and sucks up paint, making it difficult to get a nice finish. A coat or two of shellac mixed half and half with its thinner helps to stop this. Rub with steel wool to smooth before painting.

Shellac is a handy, quick varnish but, because of its **semisolubility** in water, it gets **sticky** when handled.

Fine brushes

Striping and lining need special brushes. The MACK™ liner and broad stripers are the best.

Quills

Once made of real bird quills and named for them (such as crow, thrush, etc.), they now have numbers; but they are still great brushes for decorating.

Liners

A good sable liner is wonderful to use. Artificial hair is less costly but also less efficient.

Natural-bristle brushes are traditional and, though lately we have developed plastics to look like bristles, the synthetic bristles are just not the same. I have bought some synthetic-hair brushes on occasions, but I've never found them to be satisfactory!

See more on caring for your brushes and paint on the following two pages.

Bristle brushes

Brushes are tools. Buy the best brush that you can possibly afford. A good brush, well cared for, will last a very long time.

Brush size

A two-inch brush is big enough for even large jobs. A one-inch is handy for tight spots. Although brushes are called by their width, they are different in thickness and hair length. The red-handled brush above is less tiring to use than the blue-handled one even though the work may take a bit longer.

Caring for Your Brushes and Paint

Brush care

The idea that brush care is difficult and that every time you do another job the only sensible way to get a clean brush is to buy a new one is as wrongheaded as is it wasteful.

Brushes have to be nurtured and familiar to you if nice work is what you want. Brushes are workers, and like any worker they will perform well if they are used well, properly trained, and not expected to do things that strain or injure their abilities.

Buying brushes

Buy good-quality brushes. Pick the best you can buy. Don't be fooled by fancy packaging, though; you'll be throwing that away.

Take the brush out of the wrapping before buying it; if the clerk won't let you do this, go somewhere else.

Check all the parts of the brush to see that they are firm. See that the bristles are lined up nicely. Check that the ferrule is true (the **ferrule** is the metal part that holds the bristles).

Try the brush on your hand or some other exposed skin. Does it feel as though the paint will be full of lines because the brush is hard and stiff, or will the soft hairs not be able to spread the paint without wilting?

Imagine the paint—will you be using it for thick or thin paint?

Is the handle good to hold or too thick or too thin, too short or too long?

Most reputable brand names do make good brushes, but mistakes still happen!

Preparing brushes for oil

When you get the brush home, soak it in **linseed oil.** Put it in a dish and cover the whole thing in oil—raw linseed oil.

After a few days, take it out and wipe it all off with turpentine or thinner. Wash the bristles in thinner.

Run a tap with warm water; squirt a little washing-up liquid into the bristles. Holding the handle in one hand, work the bristles into the palm of your other hand in a circular motion. Get a good lather going. Add more detergent if needed. When the oil is removed from the bristles, rinse. Rub the brush in a circular movement on a bar of white soap. Work up a good lather on your hand and then rinse. Set the hairs by shaping them to a good neat array—nothing sticking out or out of line.

Put the brush to dry where the hairs are not contacting anything else. The hole in the handle is for hanging it up—use a long nail so that the bristles don't contact the wall and become distorted.

Inexpensive Paint

Always check the sale and "whoops-we-made-a-mistake" (boo-boo) items in paint stores. The general population has an abysmal sense of color and one can often get great colors for next to nothing. What most people don't realize is that nothing is anything until you put something next to it. So with colors, so with everything.

To keep all brushes well, do this after every use.

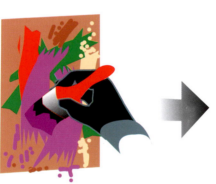

Pick a spot that won't annoy others or yourself as a paint knocking-out place—a corner of the shed or a rough piece of board.

When you have finished painting your project, paint away on the knocking-out area until very little paint remains in the brush.

Swish the brush in solvent. This step will be familiar but, if you have knocked-out, there will be much less to wash out.

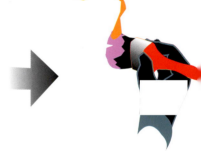

Squirt a little dishwashing detergent onto the bristles.

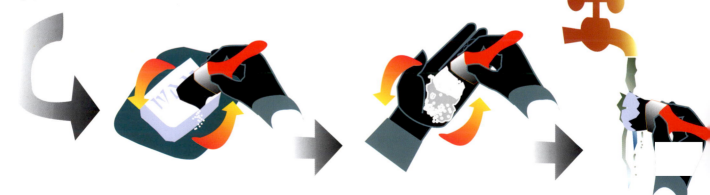

Take a bar of white soap and rub the brush around on it to make a lather. The soap helps restore some needed oils to the bristles.

Rub the brush around on the palm of your other hand, returning to the soap bar or rinsing as needed, until a good lather fills the bristles.

Rinse in warm water. Shake or whirl most of the water out.

Leftover paint

People like you and me often find that they have some paint left in the can after a job that might be useful later. The problem is that paint has stuff in it to make it dry that works when it comes into contact with oxygen (air). When you close a can, some air stays in with the leftover paint. The paint that is close to this air starts drying and a skin is formed. Shake the can— the theory is that by shaking the can (after the lid is firmly on), little bubbles of air form, causing the paint to thicken a little throughout and leaving less skin-forming oxygen in the remaining space. I sometimes do this— it makes me feel knowledgable—but by the time I've got another paint pot out to do something, I can never remember which cans have received this treatment; so I've no way of checking its efficacy. There are some who say, "Never shake a can of paint!" Take my advice—*never* take advice that contains the word *never*.

Skinning

Before using leftover paint, take the skin off. Scrape the oily stuff from the bottom of the skin back into the paint and stir it up. Throw the skin away.

Leftover paint tends to dry slower than freshly opened paint because some of the ingredients that help it to dry have been used up forming a skin.

Straining paint

Skin that has broken up as you try to remove it should be strained out. Paper strainers are cheap; so have a few handy.

Get a clean, dry can such as a coffee can. Put the strainer in the top. Pour some paint into the strainer—no more than about halfway up the side of the funnel. With a smallish brush push the paint against the cloth strainers. Stir gently until you have enough for your job. If you then have any left over, don't put it back in the original can or you will have to strain it again next time.

Needed next day

Many times you may want to keep a brush moist for the next day. Put the brush in a small can of solvent. Standing the brush in the can of solvent will not permanently bend the ends of the bristles *if there is plenty of solvent*—probably as much as up to the top of the ferrule. Don't keep the brush in the freezer—tried it—awful!

Rub the brush in circles on the palm of your other hand. Rinse your hand when too sudsy. Rinse the brush with warm water (not hot) as needed.

Keep doing this, adding a few more drops of detergent until the suds are white.

Rinse under a running tap or in a bucket of warm water. The detergent takes out oils that keep the brush supple; next we will put a little back.

Go to the next row down, far left.

Set the bristles straight and true. The newer the brush, the more you will need to train the hairs this way.

Hang the brush in a dry place on a long nail. Don't paint with oil paint until the water has all gone from the bristles—in other words, *till it's dry.*

Brushes get better and better as they get used—if you care for them.

Don't let anyone tell you to buy a brush and throw it away after use; this is a terrible waste of money and materials, and it means that you are always having a hard time because you are always working with a "raw" brush.

Even if you believe in a challenge, remember that any damned fool can rough it!

Andrew's
SLOOP SLEIGH

Sloop sleighs, pulled by a team of two horses, were once an everyday sight for young children, and that's why Mike Smith's dad made him a toy one back in the 1920s. When I saw Mike's sleigh just a few years ago, I wanted to make one for my son, Andrew, who was three at the time.

Mike's sleigh was made of anything his dad could get—bent nails, odd pieces of wood, tin cans for shoeing. Andrew's sleigh is made from store-bought materials, but gives just as much pleasure to the maker and fun to the child.

This is the Gore Bay mail sleigh. It carried the mail across the frozen North Channel of Lake Huron. It has a long pin in the evener that joins the horses to the sleigh so that the driver can set the horses free, thus saving them, if the ice cracked, from sinking with the sleigh!

Historic villages and maple sugar camps often offer winter hayrides. The vehicle they use is generally a sloop sleigh; so if you want to get a good look at one, a pioneer museum is where to go. In the country you will sometimes see old sloop sleighs rotting where they were left after their last day's work, many years ago.

When you are building something, such as this child's sleigh, it's good to know what the real thing looks like, because it cannot be made exactly the same. Occasionally you will have to make an allowance for the fact that your sleigh is made from different materials from the original full-size one and that it will be subjected to different stresses. This sounds a bit serious, but don't worry about it enough to put you off. Here's what you do—if something that

you are building seems too chunky, make it lighter; if it breaks—fix it!

You are not going to be able to do this work first off. Nobody can. Don't believe what you see on TV; think about what you don't see. You don't see mistakes, you don't see the time it takes for real things to be made, you don't ever see anybody pondering what to do next or wondering if the next move could somehow be improved—**you don't see nothing!**

Let's talk about the sleigh now.

There are three main parts to the sloop sleigh—two **bobs** and one **body.**

Each bob has two **runners** joined by a **lower bunk,** an **upper bunk,** and a **roller.** The hind bob has a chain at each end of its roller. These are to make the bobs follow. The fore bob roller has a pole fixed at its center for pulling. The body is a box with a floor.

Easy.

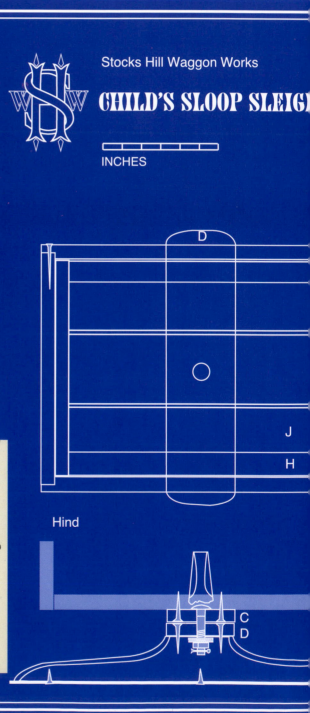

Stocks Hill Waggon Works

CHILD'S SLOOP SLEIGH

INCHES

D

O

J

H

Hind

C
D

EATON Sloop Sleigh

38 50 Freight Paid

A splendid quality, easy-running Sleigh at a very reasonable price. Built for long service and hard working conditions. Specially selected materials of extra quality are used in the construction, and its correct proportions and design make this sloop sleigh one of the best procurable. Has steel shoes, oak runners, benches and bolsters are hard maple and birch, poles are oak. Bolster stakes are 40 inches apart. We can supply 42-inch bolsters if wanted. Substantially braced and well ironed throughout. Handsomely finished and well painted in red, and varnished.

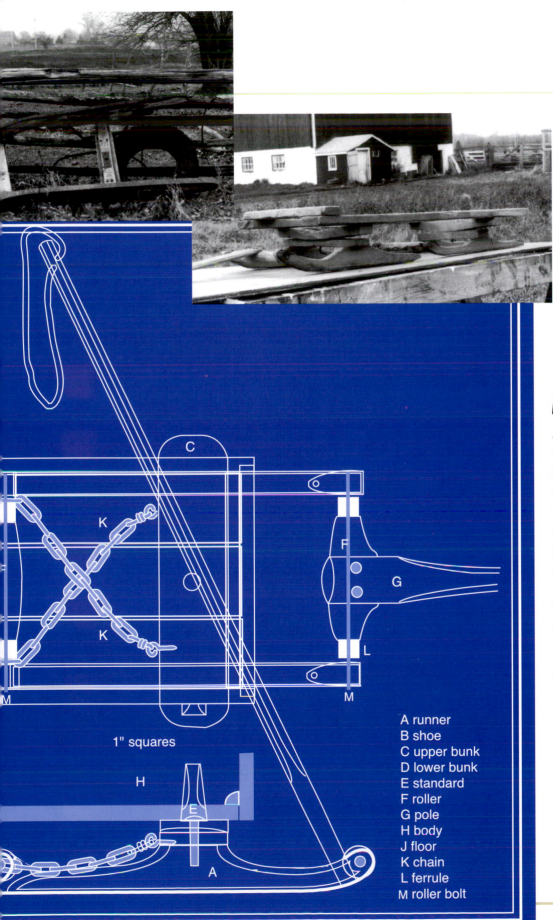

Old sleighs are often found in fields just junked after their last trip. Some farmers are using them again because a team and sleigh beats a tractor any deep-snow day.

This is a photo of Mike's sleigh, the inspiration for Andrew's.

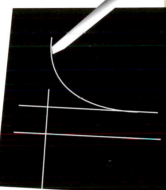

Go into any shop where hand work is done, and you will see pieces of shaped cardboard or thin wood hanging on the walls. These are **templates**. Templates are used to mark out a job without the necessity of using paper plans, which would soon deteriorate. Information such as distances from other templates when making something is often written on the template.

Paper plans didn't even exist for most of the carriages that were built. The new vehicle was drawn full size on a blackboard and the craftsmen made templates from this chalk drawing. When they needed the board for something else, it was wiped cleaned!

Working this way is good in many ways. The information gets into your head, where it will work when you are not working. It's in a place where it can be worked on as well as influence other data that your senses bring into your life.

Do a full-size drawing of the sleigh from this blueprint. From it you will get an idea of its size. If you are using chalk, watch out for rain!

Constructing the sloop sleigh is detailed in the following 14 pages.

1" squares

A runner
B shoe
C upper bunk
D lower bunk
E standard
F roller
G pole
H body
J floor
K chain
L ferrule
M roller bolt

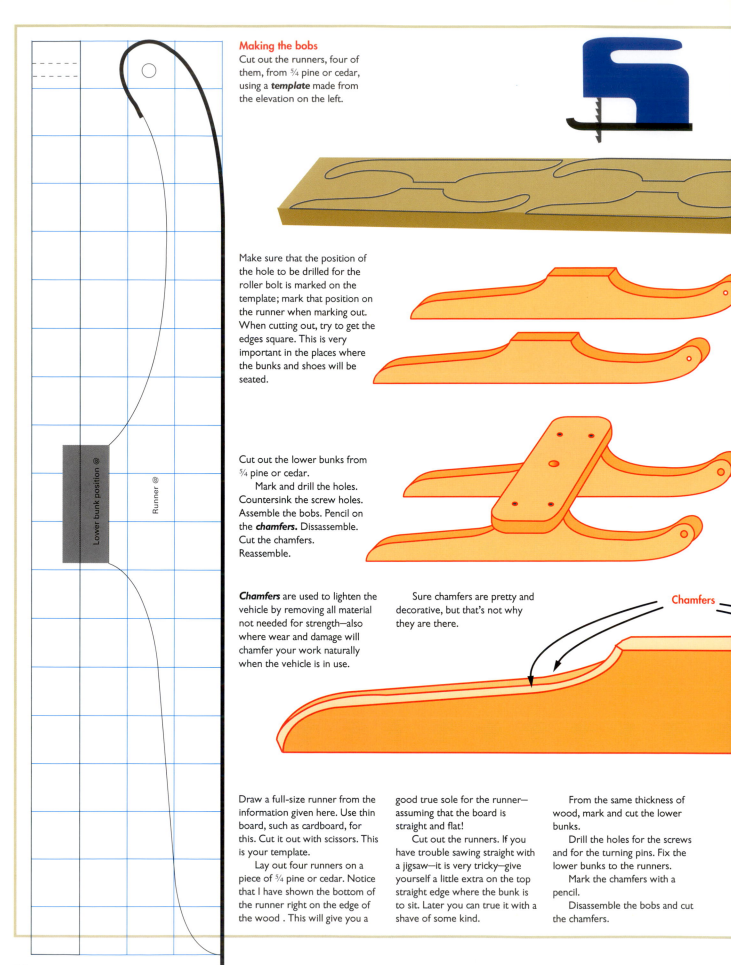

Lower bunk position @

Runner @

Making the bobs

Cut out the runners, four of them, from ⁵⁄₄ pine or cedar, using a **template** made from the elevation on the left.

Make sure that the position of the hole to be drilled for the roller bolt is marked on the template; mark that position on the runner when marking out. When cutting out, try to get the edges square. This is very important in the places where the bunks and shoes will be seated.

Cut out the lower bunks from ⁵⁄₄ pine or cedar.

Mark and drill the holes. Countersink the screw holes. Assemble the bobs. Pencil on the **chamfers.** Dissassemble. Cut the chamfers. Reassemble.

Chamfers are used to lighten the vehicle by removing all material not needed for strength—also where wear and damage will chamfer your work naturally when the vehicle is in use.

Sure chamfers are pretty and decorative, but that's not why they are there.

Chamfers

Draw a full-size runner from the information given here. Use thin board, such as cardboard, for this. Cut it out with scissors. This is your template.

Lay out four runners on a piece of ⁵⁄₄ pine or cedar. Notice that I have shown the bottom of the runner right on the edge of the wood . This will give you a good true sole for the runner—assuming that the board is straight and flat!

Cut out the runners. If you have trouble sawing straight with a jigsaw—it is very tricky—give yourself a little extra on the top straight edge where the bunk is to sit. Later you can true it with a shave of some kind.

From the same thickness of wood, mark and cut the lower bunks.

Drill the holes for the screws and for the turning pins. Fix the lower bunks to the runners.

Mark the chamfers with a pencil.

Disassemble the bobs and cut the chamfers.

Andrew's Sloop Sleigh

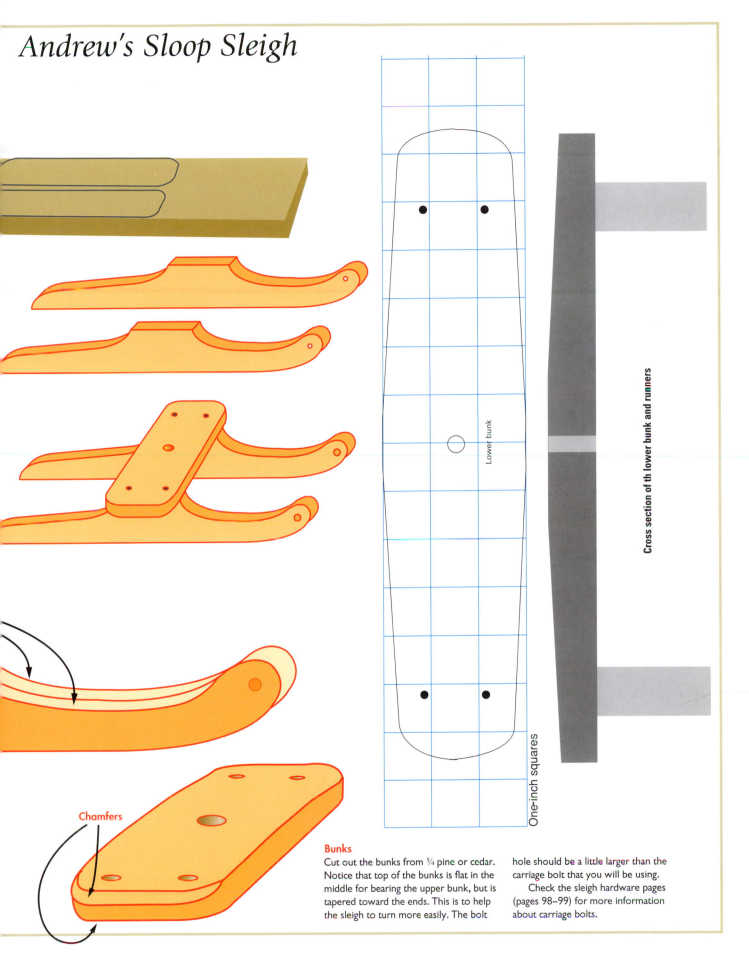

Lower bunk

One-inch squares

Cross section of th lower bunk and runners

Chamfers

Bunks

Cut out the bunks from ⁵⁄₄ pine or cedar. Notice that top of the bunks is flat in the middle for bearing the upper bunk, but is tapered toward the ends. This is to help the sleigh to turn more easily. The bolt hole should be a little larger than the carriage bolt that you will be using.

Check the sleigh hardware pages (pages 98–99) for more information about carriage bolts.

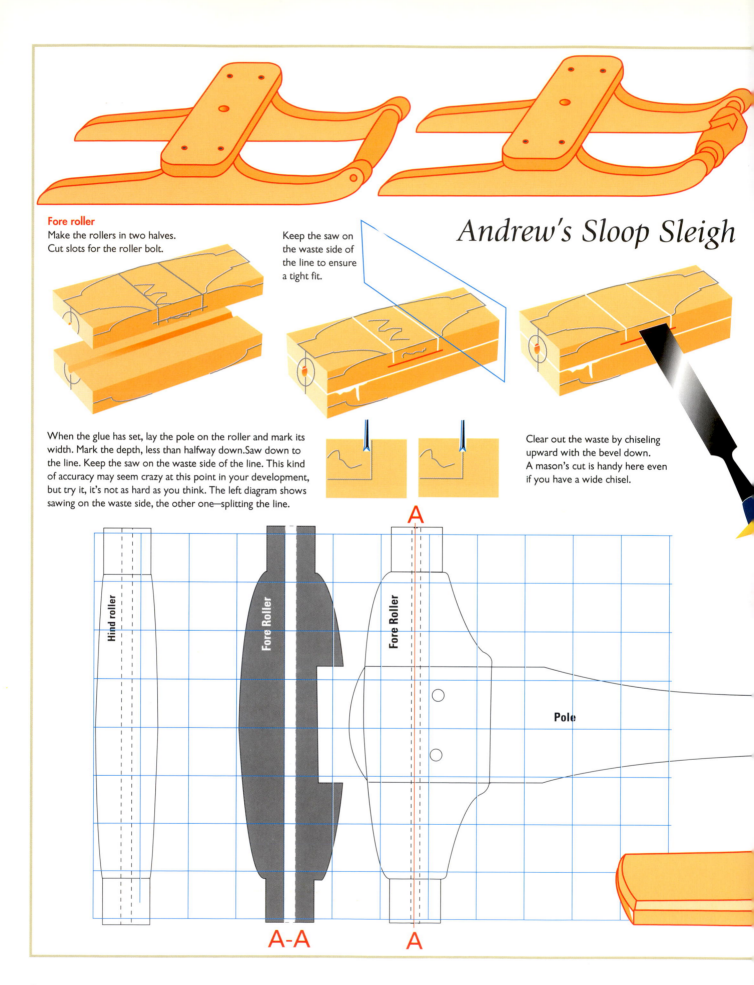

Andrew's Sloop Sleigh

Fore roller

Make the rollers in two halves. Cut slots for the roller bolt.

Keep the saw on the waste side of the line to ensure a tight fit.

When the glue has set, lay the pole on the roller and mark its width. Mark the depth, less than halfway down. Saw down to the line. Keep the saw on the waste side of the line. This kind of accuracy may seem crazy at this point in your development, but try it, it's not as hard as you think. The left diagram shows sawing on the waste side, the other one—splitting the line.

Clear out the waste by chiseling upward with the bevel down. A mason's cut is handy here even if you have a wide chisel.

Hind roller

Fore Roller

Fore Roller

A

A

A-A

A

Pole

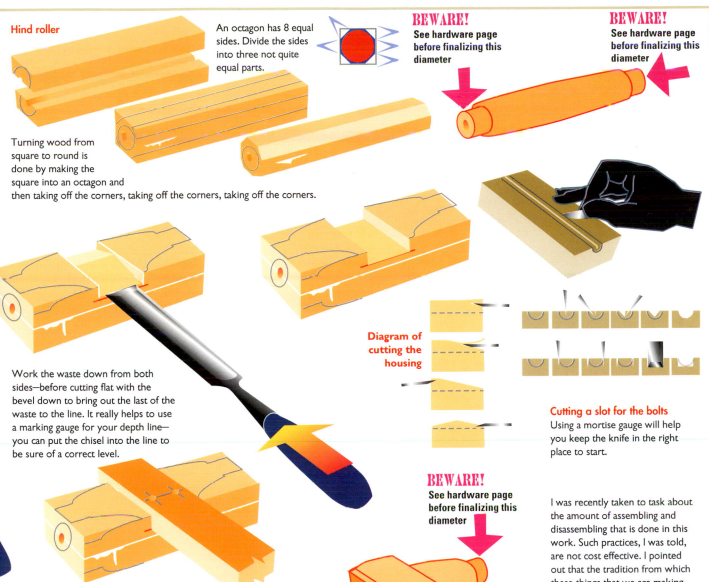

Hind roller

An octagon has 8 equal sides. Divide the sides into three not quite equal parts.

BEWARE! See hardware page before finalizing this diameter

BEWARE! See hardware page before finalizing this diameter

Turning wood from square to round is done by making the square into an octagon and then taking off the corners, taking off the corners, taking off the corners.

Work the waste down from both sides—before cutting flat with the bevel down to bring out the last of the waste to the line. It really helps to use a marking gauge for your depth line—you can put the chisel into the line to be sure of a correct level.

Diagram of cutting the housing

Cutting a slot for the bolts

Using a mortise gauge will help you keep the knife in the right place to start.

BEWARE! See hardware page before finalizing this diameter

I was recently taken to task about the amount of assembling and disassembling that is done in this work. Such practices, I was told, are not cost effective. I pointed out that the tradition from which these things that we are making come expects things to last a lot longer than anything made recently; so what is cost effective?

Old time Salesman: This waggon will be good for a hundred years!

Customer: That's as may be, but will it last?

To drill a hole straight through the rollers is difficult; so they are made in two pieces. Mark up and cut out the blanks, and cut a slot with a pocket knife. The bolt that goes through the rollers is round but this doesn't mean that the hole must be round. For a ¼" bolt, a slot in each roller piece ¼" wide and ⅛" deep is good. Then the bottom of the slot can be cleaned out with a ¼" chisel.

Lay out the pole and cut it out. Trim the sides square where they will be contacting the roller. After gluing the fore roller together mark the pole

BEWARE! See hardware page before finalizing this diameter

width on it and cut the housing slot (dado).

Put the pole in the housing and make sure it is snug. Mark where the two carriage bolts are to be. Check that the hole will be forward of the fore roller bolt. Center-punch the hole when you have decided where it

should be. To ensure correct replacement make some pencil marks crossing both pieces. Remove the pole and drill the holes. Reseat the pole. Drill down through the roller and secure with carriage bolts. Disassemble and shape the fore roller and pole.

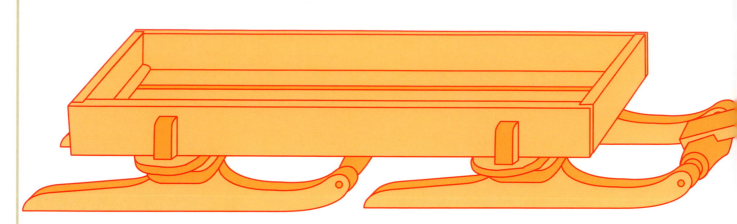

Body

The width of the body is determined by measuring the floor boards plus the ¼"–⅜" gap between them (the gap is to let the snow out). Don't rush into this; if it seems a bit tricky for you, think about it. Make your own diagrams. There is no hurry. Look at the plans in the intro (pages 90–91).

Lay the floorboards on the assembled bobs to get an idea of the finished sleigh.

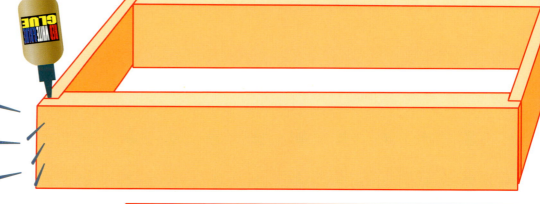

Make a box with rabbet or lap joint corners. Glue and dovetail nail with 2" finishing nails.

At each end inside, nail a length of quarter-round molding one floorboard thickness up from the bottom.

Put the floor in position and nail through the ends to secure it.

Mark the position of the bunks. Drill a ¾" hole ¼" deep where the heads of the carriage bolts will be.

Attach the upper bunks. Set all nail heads.

Andrew's sloop sleigh

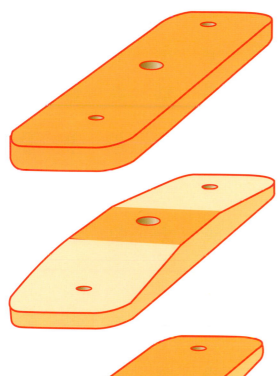

Standards

On a real wagon or sleigh the *standards* hold the body in position and provide rings for tying the load. These standards are just for looks. Fix them to the body with finishing nails; they have to come off for painting, so don't fix them too well.

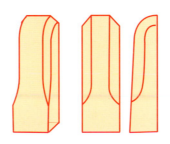

Upper bunks

Cut the upper bunks from 1" stock. Shape as shown in the section and plan. Notice that the upper bunks are flat on top and tapered on the bottom.

You might like to chamfer some of the upper bunk; I'll let you decide where to do that.

Nail setting

Nails are pushed below the surface of the wood using a *nail set.* These come in several sizes at the hardware or tool store.

Hammer the nail in as close to the surface as you can without denting the wood with the hammer. Place the nail set on the nail head, and tap it down below the surface—about the depth of the head.

Fill the hole with wood filler of some kind and smooth off.

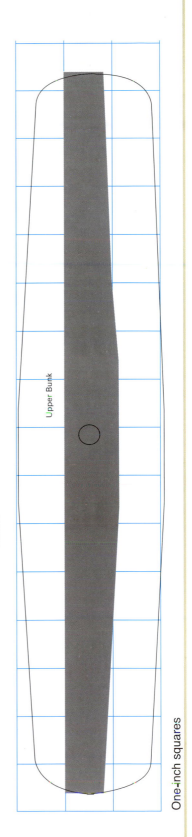

Upper Bunk

One-inch squares

CHILD'S SLOOP SLEIGH

INCHES

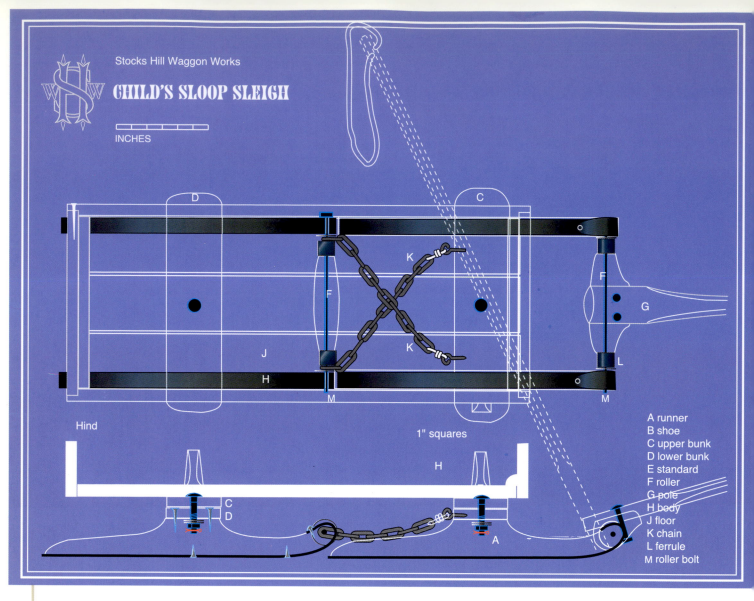

Hind

1" squares

D

C

F

G

J

H

M

K

K

F

L

M

C
D

H

A

A runner
B shoe
C upper bunk
D lower bunk
E standard
F roller
G pole
H body
J floor
K chain
L ferrule
M roller bolt

Carriage bolts

Easily recognized by the square shank behind the domed head, the **carriage bolt** is an efficient fastener and fun to work with. These special bolts come in increments of ¼" length and ¹⁄₁₆" diameter.

The length is measured from behind the head to the far end of the threading. If you are joining two pieces of wood that have a total thickness of 1½", a 2" bolt will be needed. Once these bolts were made with the thread only partway up the shank. Nowadays the threading is all the way up.

Washers

Put a washer on before the nut when working with wood. This stops the nut from biting into the wood. Two washers on the bob bolts here help turning.

Phillips   Slot   Robertson

Nuts

Until recently, because they are easier to make, all nuts were square. If you want to make something look old, such as this sleigh, use square nuts.

Screws

The main difference with screws is in the head. The shape of the head and the shape of the hole or groove in it help you put the screw into the wood. **Slot screws** are the traditional screw type; to drive one, you should use a screwdriver that fits snug into the slot.

Many people don't do this and the smaller screwdriver rips up the slot—messy business. For old-looking work that has exposed screw heads, use the slots.

Phillips screws, with a cross on top, probably evolved from **Chicago screws** (still the nickname for nails in some parts!). In Canada the **Robertson** or **square-socket screw** is more abundant. Robertsons are wonderful and I use them most of the time. The Robertson has different sizes of socket; for us the medium is usual for the No. 8 screws we use.

Screwing & countersinking

By the book   Usual method

Head shapes vary. Go to your local store and look at them. Some heads are **domed-round,** some are **rounded flat-pan,** some are **half-round (oval),** others are **countersunk.** This last one, countersunk, is the one we are using most of the time in this book.

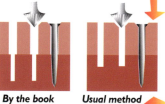

Ferrules

Wood splits, and in places where this is likely to happen, we protect it with a metal sleeve called a **ferrule**. The ferrule should be tight on the wood if it is to be effective.

To achieve the tightest possible fit, the metal is expanded by heating and then shrunk onto the wood. Here's how it is done.

Take the ferrule that you will be using; I sawed off about an inch from the metal pipe that was once part of an office chair. File the edges smooth and square. Take off any burrs. Measure the inside of the ferrule.

Cut the wood where the ferrule is to be seated to a diameter slightly larger than the inside measurement of the ferrule. There is not much difference between the two and there is no way to tell you what it will be. If it is too big, however, this will become apparent after a few tries and, if it is too small, wrap a piece of heavy brown paper around the wood and try again. Heat the ferrule; this will make it expand. Put the ferrule onto the wood, and quench it by pouring water over it. The ferrule will contract and become tight on the wood. When heating the ferrule, do **not** heat it red hot. Very, very warm is what it should be. Hotter than this and it will burn the wood.

Andrew's Sloop Sleigh

Shoeing

Mike's sleigh had cookie-tin shoes. Today aluminum siding or 30-gauge sheet metal works fine. The shoes should be at least $\frac{1}{16}$" wider than the runner. This is to prevent wear to the wooden runner. To measure for your shoes, pin a strip of paper at the spot where the shoe starts, and wrap it around to the end just as you will be doing with the metal shoe. The first screw, in the top of the runner, is a round-head; the others are pan-head. They will soon wear down smooth when in use.

Pole and fore roller

Two carriage bolts secure the pole to housing in the fore roller.

Notice how the square shank of the carriage bolts bites into the wood and stops rotation.

Fitting carriage bolts

When using carriage bolts, drill a hole the size of the bolt, e.g., $\frac{1}{4}$" bolt = $\frac{1}{4}$" hole. This gives a tight fit as the threads are wider than the shank. Hammer the bolt in, and tighten the nut onto the washer. The bolts betwixt and between the bunks are loose-fitting and not tightened. To keep the washers and nuts from straying, either drill a small hole and insert a split pin or,

and this is easier, make a saw cut with a hacksaw, vertically down the end of the threads a little way; then, after the nut is in position, pry the cut apart a bit.

Rollers and chains

A $\frac{1}{4}$" rod (roller bolt) goes through each of the rollers. Between the roller and the hind runner there is a chain link and a washer. The outside of the roller bolt is secured by a nut.

Choose a nice piece of chain; it will be taking quite a strain. Tie the chain to the eye bolts with leather. The chain should hang down, but not quite touch the ground when the runners are in the straight position.

Andrew's Sloop Sleigh

Everything is here but the sides.

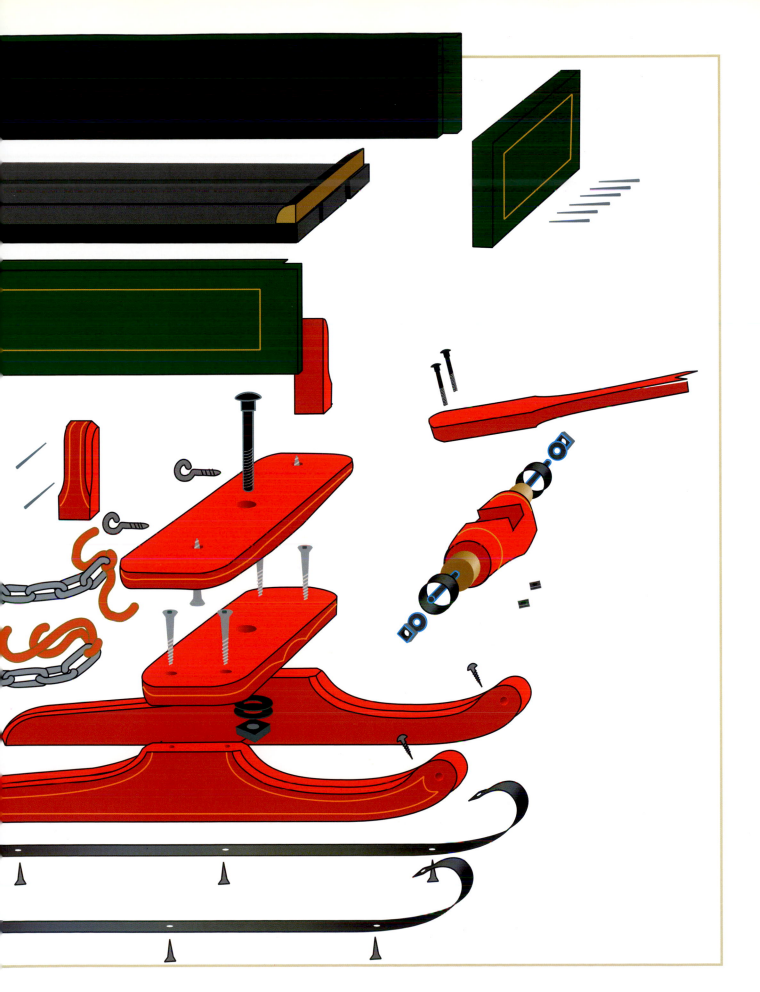

Andrew's Sloop Sleigh

Mike's sleigh was a toy; so is Andrew's. But if you want to make your sleigh into a real sleigh to grow into, modify it by adding sides and by making the pole longer.

Sides

Get some ½" wood four inches wide, and cut it to the length of the **box.** Shape the ends to your liking.

In the cross section on the **blueprint** (at the top pf page 103) you will see that the outside of the side is flush with the box side.

Supports

The indent in the **supports** is as deep as the difference in thickness between the side and the box side. For example, if the box side is ¾" actual and the side is ½" actual, then the indent will be ¾" – ½" = ¼".

The rear supports are sloped off to make the rider's back support—called the **lazy back**—more comfortable—notice that you will need to make a **left** and a **right** version of these.

Assembly

The supports are joined to the box side with a screw. Their position is in line with the standards so that if the screw goes through the box side, it will go into the standard.

When you have fixed the support to the box, lay the sides in place and mark the positions for the screws. Take the sides to your work area and drill the pilot holes. Fix the sides to the supports, leaving about a pencil thickness of space between the side and the box side. This is to let the snow out.

Lazy back

Cut a piece of 1" plank to fit between the sides. The height and shape of the top is up to you. Screw it to the rear supports.

Pole

For adults to pull, the pole should be longer. Try a few lengths and make it as long as possible without its becoming inconvenient; then, when your children or grand-children are ready to take over, cut some off for them.

Or make a series of poles; why not—you're a sleigh builder now!

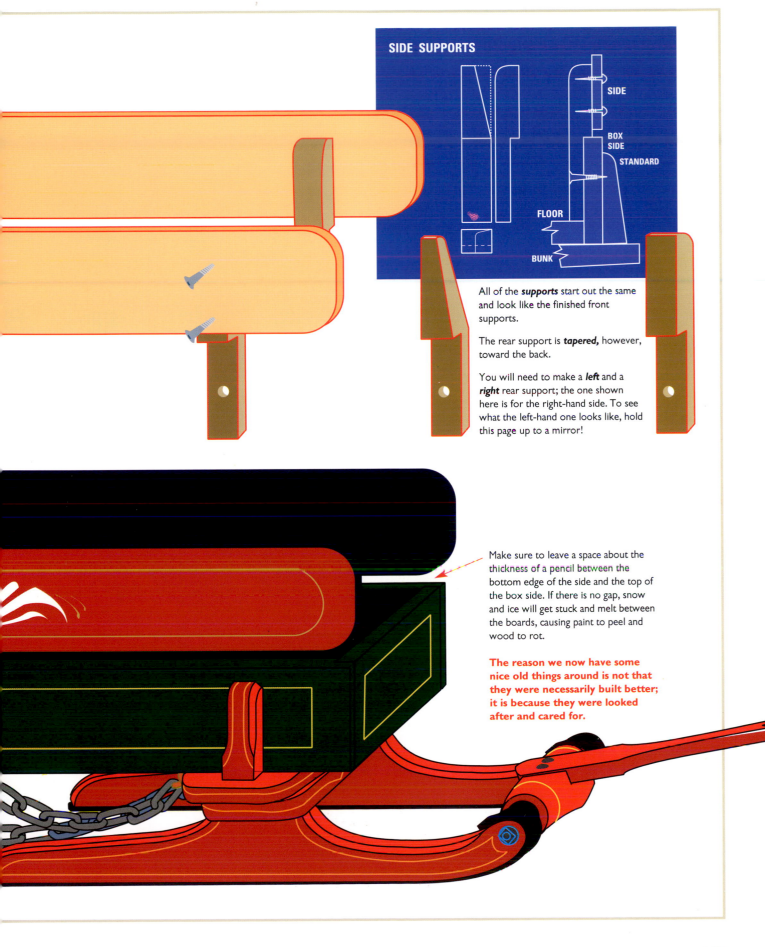

SIDE SUPPORTS

SIDE

BOX SIDE

STANDARD

FLOOR

BUNK

All of the **supports** start out the same and look like the finished front supports.

The rear support is **tapered,** however, toward the back.

You will need to make a **left** and a **right** rear support; the one shown here is for the right-hand side. To see what the left-hand one looks like, hold this page up to a mirror!

Make sure to leave a space about the thickness of a pencil between the bottom edge of the side and the top of the box side. If there is no gap, snow and ice will get stuck and melt between the boards, causing paint to peel and wood to rot.

The reason we now have some nice old things around is not that they were necessarily built better; it is because they were looked after and cared for.

Painting the sleigh

Good painting needs a good foundation. This means a smooth and even surface free of any unneeded dents, dings, or scratches. This is not just because someone gets fussy and likes it that way; it has its origin in practicality.

Water is the big enemy of paint and wood. Water rots wood and, though we try to protect the wood with paint, this can sometimes work in the opposite way. Paint is not absolutely waterproof, and moisture travels through it; a layer of paint not properly adhered to the wood will hold water in the space between.

Water is encouraged to leave as quickly as possible, and anything that helps water to stay is not good. Dents, dings, and scratches are great harbors for water—**stop** them.

Stopping

Plastic wood, surfacing putty, old-fashioned putty—try them out—if you like one, use it.

Fill (stop) all exposed countersunk screws, set nails, bad joins, hammer dents, holes, chips, gashes, slivers, and such. Sand smooth.

Knot sealing

Knots have lots of resin in them that can bleed through and mark any paint that has been put over them. Dab a couple of coats of **shellac** on any knots to seal them.

Primer

Special paints help paint adhere to the base material. Because these paints are put on first, they are called **prime coats.** Wood and metal require different primers.

You may like to use a spray can of red oxide or gray metal primer as the amount of metal in these projects is very small. The fine spray that one gets from a spray can produces a very pleasant, smooth, thin coat. If you don't want to use—or, like me, generally can't afford—spray cans, brush-on primer is the thing to use.

Wood primer is generally white. When wood primer dries, it has a kind of chalkiness that sands to a very smooth finish, forming a good foundation for top coats. Years ago, wood primer had to be left at least 48 hours before top-coating, but I think today you can top-coat as soon as the primer is dry; even so, I leave the prime coat two days—slows me down, gives me time to think.

Applying paint

Painting needs just as much effort as the work that has gone before it. It requires physical and mental effort and skills. Painters who say, "My, isn't this fun!" need not apply.

Sailing is quite like painting. A lot of folk, when invited out, imagine a languid cruise, tranquil and serene. In reality the best thing about it is the reminiscing later.

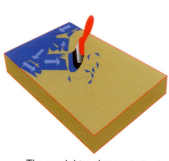

The good thing about painting is that it's a solitary pursuit; there are no two-handled brushes—if anyone ever designs one, watch the divorce rate climb!

Andrew's Sloop Sleigh

Schedule of painting

Disassemble the sleigh.	No need to take everything apart; just separate into the groups of parts as shown.
Prime all metal parts and let dry.	Chains may be painted if you wish. Prime any screw and bolt heads that have not been stopped.
Seal knots with shellac.	Two coats will be dry in less than an hour.
Prime all wood parts.	Use your newer brushes to wear and train them; then they will become older, better, best brushes.
Give a very light sand.	This will make it easier to see where the second primer coat is needed.
Reprime all the wood.	
Sand smooth with 120-grit.	Old 80-grit paper will do. On new paper watch out for nibs. Remove them by rubbing two sheets together face to face.
Tint coat (optional).	Mix together half primer and half the top-coat color.
Sand.	
Paint the floor (top & bottom), inside the box, and the top edges.	
Top-coat all parts that are not the box.	
Paint the outside and top edge of the box.	
Next morning recoat inside box; take the rest of the day off.	
Sand with 120-grit or finer.	
Repaint all parts.	
Decorate.	After decorating you may wish to varnish everything but the inside.
Reassemble.	

Applying paint the proper way

To get paint to stay on, you have to put it on as if you mean it.

Dip into the paint about halfway up the bristles; tap it out a bit. Take the brush to the knocking-out wall and knock the paint in by brushing in all directions using a hearty and robust manner. If any hairs work loose, take them out.

Dip again into the paint—not too much, less is best. You can always put on more thin coats—wrinkling, "crizzling," and runs, the result of overloaded painting, are harder to fix.

Apply the paint to the work, brushing firmly in all directions. A hearty and enthusiatic attitude is appropriate. This way of painting can be noisy. Don't be alarmed if this is not your ordinary casual hobby. The brush has to whack the paint into all those scratches left by the sanding and get a firm grip on the previous layers.

When part of an area is more or less covered, with brush strokes in all directions, lay the paint out by brushing toward the edge. Then get back to the rest of the work, applying in all directions, and then laying out.

If you are intending to paint only two coats, then lay off both in the long direction. For more than two coats, lay off one coat longways and then the next coat sideways; repeat until the required number of coats is completed. If you are laying off both ways and painting many coats, before painting the last coat, sand flat using wet paper and water.

To get a really "deep" finish on the box, finish with at least two coats of varnish. For the first coat of varnish mix about one-quarter volume of body color to the varnish. Rub out wet. Then add a coat of clear varnish. Decorate and varnish again.

Disassembly for painting

Take the sleigh apart for painting, leaving groups such as the bobs and pole together.

Colors

Bobs are usually red or dark red.

The box can be dark green, black, dark blue, red—anything mature, elegant, and not liable to startle the horses!

Areas that may become dirtied with grease when in use are painted black. For example, the roller ends.

Stencils

Push some paint through a hole in something else and you've got stenciling. Stenciling is a simple method of repeating a motif many times.

Prepared paper is the easiest to use, and it lasts. Take a piece of heavy paper; cardboard is too thick. Coat the paper with several layers of shellac, both sides. When dry, draw on the design you wish to repeat. Make sure to leave a good wide border.

Lay the paper on a piece of glass, and with a knife cut out the voids that you need. Make sure that the corners are well cut; in fact, go just a tiny bit further than the corner for crisp, clean work.

Position the stencil on the place that you wish to decorate. Fix with some masking tape.

Paint is dabbed through the holes in the stencil either by using a stencil brush or, for the inexperienced, a cloth pad. When stenciling, do not rub—dab up and down. This gives the true stenciled effect. To load a stencil brush, dab it up and down on the paint palette. Very little paint is needed.

Lining and striping

What is commonly thought of as pinstriping is not. Pinstriping refers to a pattern of cloth. Painted lines less than about ¼" are called **lining.** Painted lines above this width are called **stripes** or **broad stripes!**

Use the edge of the piece to guide your extended little finger; a little talc on your fingertip helps to slip way. Work up your Mack™ on a small palette, and let the paint firm up a bit before use.

Grip your painting wrist with your other hand for a good steady line. These brushes start the line with a point, so go back later and paint the corners with a quill.

Wipe out mistakes with a clean rag—no need for solvent. Decoration positions can be marked on paint surfaces with china-marking pencils and removed with turpentine when the paint is dry. Be patient, too, before brushing off any talc.

Scrolling

Brushes do best what they were made to do. With scrolling one has really only to set the brush in motion to get excellent results. Get a good scrolling brush and put a little paint on it. Work the brush back and forth on your palette. Notice how when you brush the surface and just the tip is touching, a thin line results. When you press down a little, the line becomes wider. Now bring the brush in like an airplane landing. Touching, touching, touching more, more down, and stop. Depending on how long your runway was, you now have a stroke like that of **A.** By doing the same thing and curving to the left or right, **B & C** appear. To get a pointy end, **D,** instead of stopping at the end, do a really short takeoff again. Practice, practice, feel good, be graceful, don't worry—these are the secrets of scrolling. One more thing: if it's just not working out, try for a while and then pack up.

Do it later, some other time.

A

B

C

D

Some Ideas About
HOLDING STUFF

When you're making something, cutting seems to be the main occupation, but, when you think about it, holding the materials steady while you use your saw or chisel or whatever runs a pretty close second!

Work that wobbles around when you try to do something is a surefire way to get frustrated.

Finishing work and gluing are other times that you'll appreciate some good holding devices. Don't be afraid to improvise—if it does the job for you, well that's okay.

The last hundred years have seen a lot of inventions to help make things. Most of them are supposed to save time and energy; but all that happens, it seems, is that one person now gets to do the work of two instead of the two having to do half the amount of work. They used to call them labor-saving devices—I like to call them labor-**slaving** devices.

Amidst all the electrical this and electrical that, though, there occasionally appears something that is a real down-to-earth help. Here's a great example—the **handy bench**. It has many names, call it what you will—it is wonderful!

My kids bought one for me one birthday years ago. I've been using it ever since. (I mentioned, on page 48, how my handy bench has just lasted for years.) The top is a bit warped, the ends are saw-marked, the frame is painted with lines and colors from many long-gone projects; but it still holds wood, it is still used as a bench, it's often used with the bench dogs for gluing, its tapering jaws work well for jigs and other devices. The plastic bench dogs that came with it are long gone—I just shaped some sticks into new bench dogs and carry on. What more can I tell you?

. . . Oh yes, it folds up and stashes away in a cupboard! I've used my bench everywhere, from teeny-tiny apartments to the wide and wonderful Canadian outdoors. If you haven't already got one, then save up and get one. And another good thing—they are not expensive! Ask for one for **your** birthday.

Bench hook

When sawing on a bench it helps to have a **bench hook.**

Make one (or two) for yourself.

I've used dowels here to join it together, but you could use screws.

Here is how the bench hook can be used . . . The hook helps you to keep the wood still, and also it saves the saw from cutting the bench.

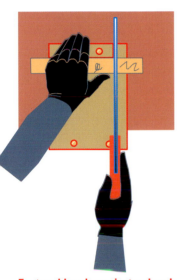

Feet and hands are just as handy as can be when you want a temporary hold on a piece of work. Using hands and feet as holding devices—with a bit of careful thought—is not anywhere near as dangerous as when using power tools. But if it doesn't feel right—don't do it!

I must confess I just don't recall what the name of this thing is! I use it often, I know what it can do, what it has a problem with, where I got it, and just about everything about it—or should say, them, because I have two—but the name . . . my guess is that it is a type of **hold-down clamp.**

What these are used for is holding work on a bench of any kind—or a on plank, if that's what you're using as a bench.

How it works is this. The round shank is loose in a hole in the bench,

Call them **C clamps** or **G cramps**—or G clamps and C cramps—it doesn't matter. (Just hold this page up to a mirror and you'll see where they get their names.) You can never have too many of these handy tools. Use them for holding pieces together when gluing or when dryfitting pieces together. They do make a nasty dent if used without some kind of protection to your wood surface; so use scraps of wood to protect the work. Nowadays some of the clamps come with soft plastic pads that are quite efficient—that is, until they get lost!

Clamps come in all sizes; the size marked on the side is the maximum thickness of work that it will hold. Don't forget that you have to allow for the scraps on each side. Some clamps have deeper thoats than others.

I find that clamps, for some reason, are often on sale. When you see some on sale, and you've some spare money, **buy them.**

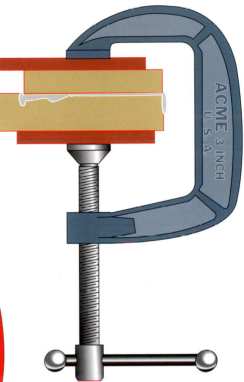

Throat

you put your workpiece under the arm, and you give the top a good whack with a **mallet** (not a hammer!). This makes the shank fit tight in the hole and so presses the arm down onto the work. While it's sometimes good to put a bit of scrap on your work to protect it, I find this tends to impare the efficiency of using these clamps; you might find that it still works just fine.

To get this device to release its grip, simply hit it (with a mallet or bit of wood) on the back corner.

Hit here with a mallet to release

Hit here with a mallet to secure

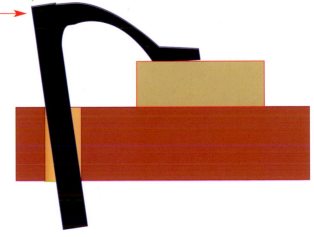

A guy I once knew said he was having trouble gluing something. He said he couldn't get a clamp strong enough to hold his work together.

My friend, Henk, says if you get into this kind of situation, it's a good indication that there is something **wrong** with your work.

Clamps are just for snuggin' it up and holding it there.

Gardener's
BUCKSAW

Even in the best of well-regulated families there are times when one just needs a little break. In our family we have a word, or rather a phrase, for too much of a good thing— "Picking up sticks." When someone needs a break, that person just quietly leaves, and if asked where they are going, the person replies, "Oh, just going to pick up a few sticks" meets with instant understanding. My father-in-law originated the term at our weekend cottage, and there, of course, he literally did pick up sticks— for kindling. Every so often he would get a really good piece that was too big to break, and so I made him this small edition of the never-popular old-fashioned bucksaw. It works perfectly on branches up to about two inches in thickness—and when not in use is nice to hang on the wall. Kids love it too, but watch out, the "Swede" saw blade is very sharp!

For small fry and small branches, fit a hacksaw blade.

The **simplest saw** that I ever heard of was an unraveled thread from a prisoner's sock that he'd dampened and coated with stone dust to cut through the bars! You can buy a special rough piece of wire from farm suppliers that rolls up in your pocket until you're ready to delimb an obstructive tree or dehorn a potentially dangerous cow.

Using this kind of "saw" for a **bow string** ("bow" as in **bow and arrow**) makes it much more controllable and easier on the hands. In England, frame saws are still called **bow saws!**

108

Frame saws

Four sticks, a blade, two nails, and a piece of string are all that is needed for a **frame saw.** No glue or fasteners of any kind are used. A frame saw is held together by the forces of nature. Frame saws are light and lovely.

You can modify this design to make any size of saw. The forces exerted on the frame are quite considerable and, though pine is fine for a saw of this size, hardwoods are better for anything larger.

How to make your own bucksaw is shown on the following two pages.

ers' Buck Saw Co©

Making the Gardener's Bucksaw

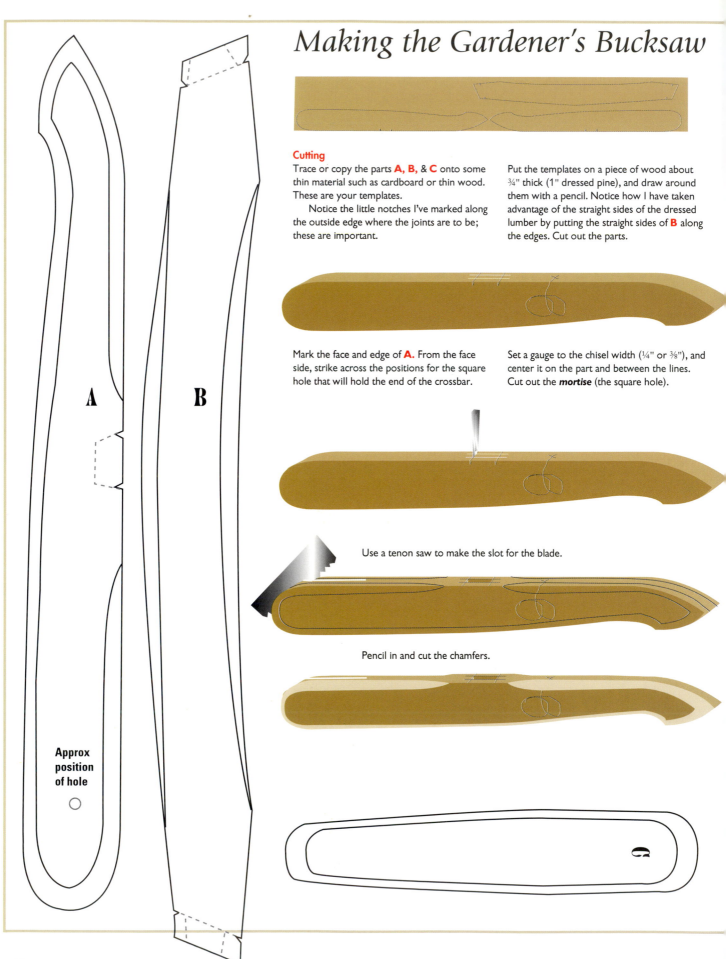

A

B

Approx position of hole

Cutting

Trace or copy the parts **A, B,** & **C** onto some thin material such as cardboard or thin wood. These are your templates.

Notice the little notches I've marked along the outside edge where the joints are to be; these are important.

Put the templates on a piece of wood about ¾" thick (1" dressed pine), and draw around them with a pencil. Notice how I have taken advantage of the straight sides of the dressed lumber by putting the straight sides of **B** along the edges. Cut out the parts.

Mark the face and edge of **A.** From the face side, strike across the positions for the square hole that will hold the end of the crossbar.

Set a gauge to the chisel width (¼" or ⅜"), and center it on the part and between the lines. Cut out the **_mortise_** (the square hole).

Use a tenon saw to make the slot for the blade.

Pencil in and cut the chamfers.

Set the **marking gauge** to the width of your chisel. Set the stock of the gauge so that the points are centered on your piece. Mark all joints using the same setting and from the same side.

Face edge

Face side

Mark and cut the little square bits **(tenons)** that are going to fit into the little square holes **(mortises).**

Pencil in and cut the chamfers.

Face and edge marking

Working on more complicated pieces, we often need some regular place that we can measure from. Woodworkers use a **whirly line (squiggle)** on the main front of pieces, and on the adjacent edge they put a **cross**—joined to the squiggle over the edge.

Use this method on this job to help get everything lined up properly.

Put the **try square** butt on the **face side** to mark squarely across the face edge. When marking the joints, use the face side for the mortise gauge stock.

Mark out and cut the **toggle.** The toggle is about ¼" thick. If you've a mind to be fancy, you can whittle the top end to something other than just plain.

Put the saw together and lay the blade on to find the position for the holes. Mark and drill small holes for the nails; for strength, get them close to the center.

Put the saw blade into the slot and push the nails through to hold it. The points of the nails may stick out the other side; snip them off with a pair of pliers or file them off.

Final assembly

With the blade pinned in the frame, lay the whole thing on a bench and wrap strong string or twine around the top ends of the uprights—the **nocks.** This does not have to be very tight—just firm. Insert the toggle and twist tight. A bit of jiggling may be needed to put the frame into the right postion when you first do this. After a while it'll be second nature.

Paint your saw red if you want to be traditional. Why **red?** It's easy to find when you leave it hanging on a tree somewhere outside where you had been working—and you will!

CHAMFERS

Most people think that chamfers are only for decoration—this is not true. Chamfers are quite functional! Come to that, all decoration is functional; but that's the "color of a different horse" that we won't go into here.

A *chamfer* is an oblique face cut into the corner (the *arris*) of a piece of wood. We have come to think that it looks pretty. It looks right. If you ask an old tradesman why he is shaving up a piece of wood he will probably say, "Because that makes it look right." After a while you'll be able to do chamfering just so that it looks right, but first we must know why chamfering is useful and beautiful.

When you make a chamfer, you remove wood. You remove the wood that you don't need; you also remove wood that would be removed later but in a random manner, i.e., from scuffs and bumps.

I worked for some years in the horse-drawn wagon business. Building wagons we needed strength for the vehicles, but we didn't need weight—to save the horse!

If the sharp corner is left on a wooden object it gets bashed and nicked, anyway. Guaranteed! The idea is to remove the sharp edge before the damage occurs.

Chamfers can make things comfortable to hold, too.

Chamfering is one of the most delightful activities in hand woodworking. It requires thought and skill, and the results are immediate. Nothing is nicer than shaving.

How to chamfer
Patience, control, and a delight in conversing with wood are all that's needed for chamfering—oh yes, and sharp tools.

Marking chamfers
Use your fingers as a guide to rough in where the chamfers are to be. These lines don't have to be accurate; they are just mnemonics.

Cutting chamfers
Drawknives are good for chamfering. They can be used bevel-down for scooping out and bevel-up for steady smoothing.

When starting a chamfer, take off just a little sliver and then increase little by little to big chunks when confident.

Take out one end as shown here, then turn the wood over, end for end, and do the other end. Smooth out the center with bevel-up, or use a spokeshave.

Chamfers are one of the few things that are fun and enjoyable to *practice.*

A mortise is a square hole in wood. To remember this name, think of the hole as a tiny grave. **Mort = dead.**

A tenon is the piece cut to fit into the mortise. To remember this name, think of the word **tenant.**

The **red-lined box** shows the boundaries of the zone where strength is needed most.

Chamfer only outside of these areas.

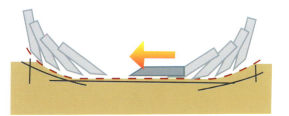

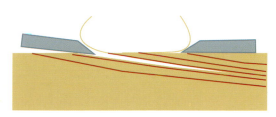

Where to chamfer

In these diagrams we can see a simple ***mortise-and-tenon joint.*** By cutting the wood away to make the ***mortise*** (square hole) and ***tenon*** (thin end that goes into the hole), we have taken away some of the strength of the wood in that area. The edge wood in these areas must remain. Away from the joints, we can take off anything that will not drastically weaken the piece.

NOTE how the cross section starts to resemble an ***octagon.*** An octagon is a square on its way to being a circle. A circle is a section of a sphere, the strongest and most natural form on Earth—and maybe elsewhere.

Grain

Chamfering can bring you into really close decision-making about which way to cut, which direction to cut, which tool to use (chamfers can also be put on with a rasp and file with much less risk than with any knife).

When making a chamfer, you will be going across the grain in both directions at the ends and with the grain or against it in between.

I've put the diagram ***above*** to show what's happening when your knife digs in and a split starts. Sharp tools help, but even these tend to dig in during an unguarded moment. If (when) a split starts, stop at once, and think about maybe shaving back the other way. The tendency of most people, including me, is to say, "No, I can pull out of it," but you can't! I know this advice will not be heeded, but don't say I didn't warn you.

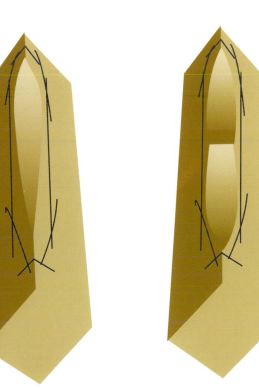

BREAST BIBS

Small pieces of wood can present a problem in shaving because the jaws of the shaving horse need to grip where you want to cut. This is where the *breast bib* comes in handy.

If you don't have a shaving horse, a breast bib is useful instead. Rest your work against a notch or a peg/nail and proceed.

The purpose of the breast bib is twofold—it protects you and your clothes from unwanted cuts and injury, and it also spreads the energy of holding a workpiece over a larger area (it works like a pad).

Breast bibs are generally about 6" square, but you can make one to whatever size suits you. Any wood will do and anything ¾" and over will work well.

To hang it around your neck, attach some cloth strips or an old belt to the back. I like to have an around-the-body strap; so if you would like one, too, fix another old belt at the bottom of the back.

The height of the bib on your body is your choice and depends on whether you are standing or sitting. For sitting down, it's best over your chest; but for standing up (using a peg), lower is often more comfortable.

Don't worry about getting things right first time. If the straps are not right for you, then change them to where you think they might be better; and if that's not comfortable, move them around until they are.

Using the breast bib

Put the work in the notch or on the peg, and rest the other end on the bib. Apply a little straight pressure to hold it firmly. Now use your drawknife or spokeshave to make the cuts you need. You can push away from you or draw toward you. When using the drawknife, the blade will cut into the bib—and you will see **why** you are wearing it!

Use your **drawknife** in either direction when working with a breast bib.

The breast bib works as an alternative to, or in conjunction with, the shaving horse.

Traditional woodworking shops had a a post or wall location with a hole where those who needed to do a bit of fine shaving would insert a hard wood peg. The woodworker would rest the work on the peg and push against it with the bib (which could

also have a peg set in it). Some of these pegs had a metal tip added by drilling a small hole, then inserting and filing off a nail to help hold the work from slipping.

Not everyone has enough space on the balcony or deck to locate a peg

like this. The **simple device** shown here can be made into a bench, or it can exist as just a plank that you sit on, resting your work against the point in the vertical bracket.

If you have a deck railing, make a hole for a peg, and sit at it to work.

A **recess** in the bib can really help to put pressure on when using a **brace and bit.**

Some Simple
CHAIRS

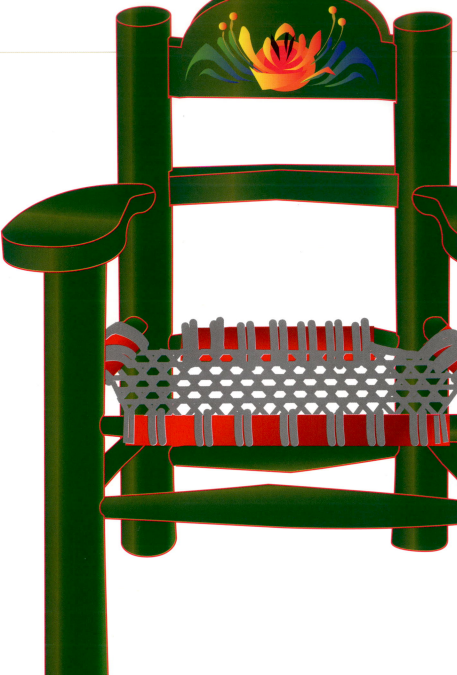

When I was about fourteen years old (some time ago), Mr. Taylor, our carpentry and joinery teacher, gave David Ridehaugh, a serious student, a set of plans for a chair. This was to be Dave's next project! I could not imagine anything more auspicious. To me, making a chair was, as we would say nowadays, "to have arrived"!

Most cultures have a special place for chairs in their social structures. Even societies that don't have any furniture at all seem to have a chair—or throne—of some sort for their most important character. Why this is I do not know; what I do know is that they are really not that hard to make and that making them is very satisfying— probably because of all the mystique attached to them!

Well, let's be no more in awe—we're going to make a chair or two, and you will never be the same again!

Directions for making a chair

Making a chair is like swimming or riding a bike. Who would ever learn to swim by learning hydro-dynamics? Who would ever imagine that a person could balance on the edge of two wheels, let alone go somewhere and enjoy it, and certainly no one rides a bike considering the exact distribution of weight! You just do it!

I'm only giving a few dimensions for this job. When I do give you a measurement, don't just accept it— think about it and ask yourself why this size and not another, should I try something bigger or smaller to get what I want, is this a misprint is this a deliberate mistake, should I take this as true because it's been used for centuries, and so on.

Be intelligent. And if you try something that doesn't work out, ask yourself why it didn't work out. Do it again; learn through your mistakes.

Wood is variable, weather is changeable, tools are different, instructions are vague; there are many reasons that things go awry, so don't blame yourself. You're not stupid, just born ignorant. It's nice not to stay that way!

One thing at a time

Do not smoke or chew gum or tobacco when working.

When you have become an experienced worker, doing these things—chewing gum, etc.—without detriment to your work is easy. Until then, abstain!

Making these simple chairs is detailed on the following 22 pages.

Making a Simple Chair

A chair is just a little platform to raise you off the ground.
The simplest kind of "little platform to raise you off the ground" is called *a stool.* Once you've made a stool, making a chair is easy. Design and make your own.

A stool with a backrest is a chair.
Even the most decorated, emblazened, and prestigious chair is no more than this.

Wobbliness in a chair is not desirable.
Steadiness gives a chair a feeling of security.
Sideways forces on a chair cause the frame to move out of square. This is called *racking.*

Extra pieces—called *rungs, rails,* or *rounds*—are added to give strength and support against *racking.*
Some chairs have flat pieces of wood built in vertically beneath the seat; these kinds of chair do not need rungs.

The seat of a chair can take many forms; *solid, slats, padded,* and so on. Each kind has its own advantages and disadvantages. The kinds shown in this book are *woven;* so the basic chair structure looks like this.

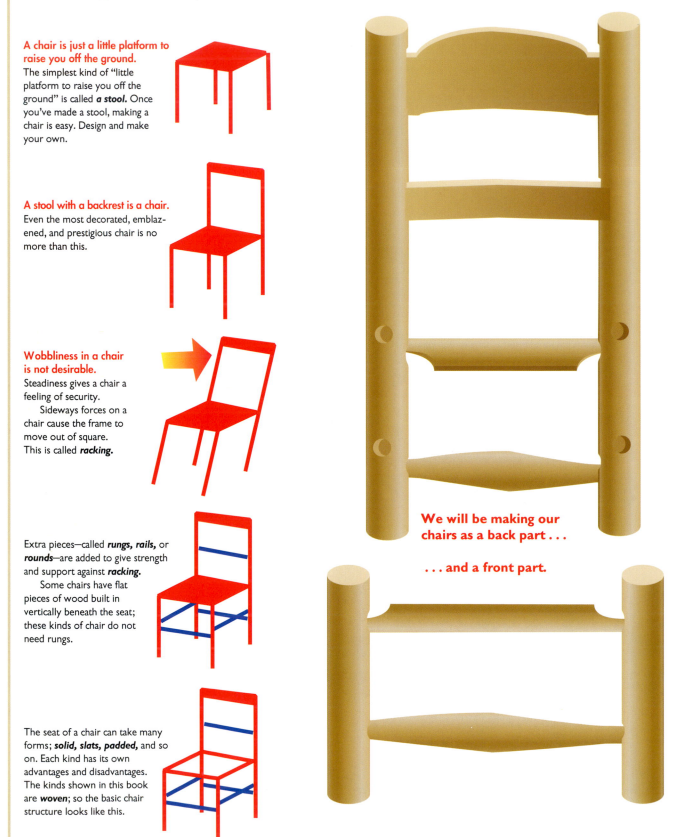

We will be making our chairs as a back part . . .

. . . and a front part.

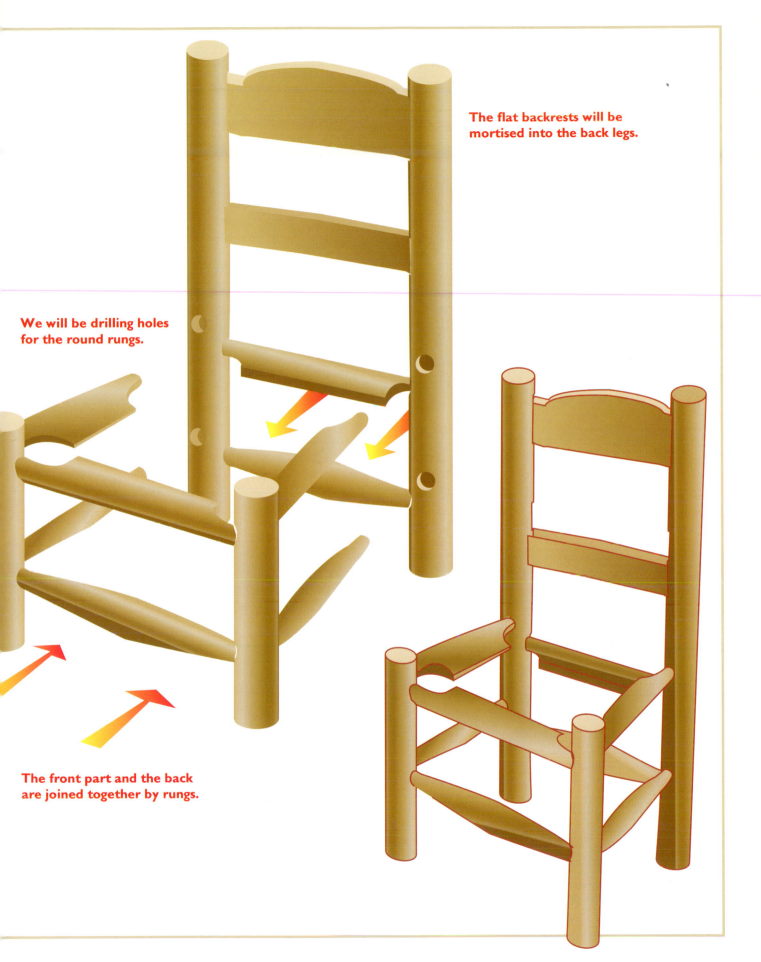

The flat backrests will be mortised into the back legs.

We will be drilling holes for the round rungs.

The front part and the back are joined together by rungs.

Making a Tiny Chair

Measurements for a tiny chair
Back legs 14" × 1¼" square
Front legs 8" × 1¼" square

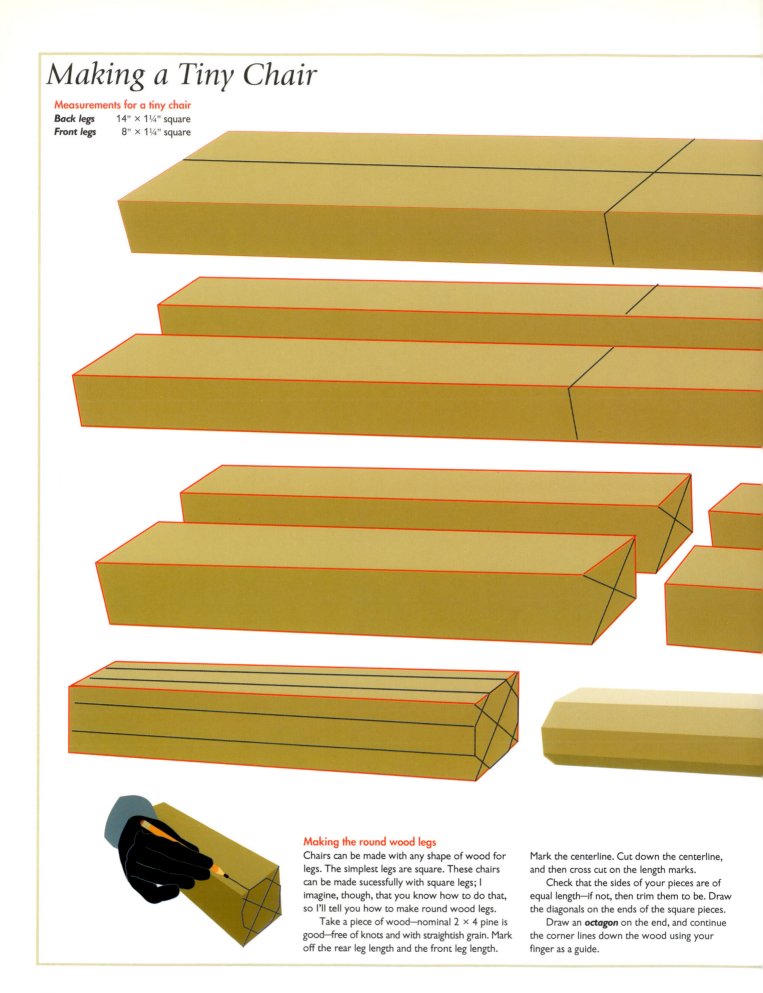

Making the round wood legs

Chairs can be made with any shape of wood for legs. The simplest legs are square. These chairs can be made sucessfully with square legs; I imagine, though, that you know how to do that, so I'll tell you how to make round wood legs.

Take a piece of wood—nominal 2 × 4 pine is good—free of knots and with straightish grain. Mark off the rear leg length and the front leg length.

Mark the centerline. Cut down the centerline, and then cross cut on the length marks.

Check that the sides of your pieces are of equal length—if not, then trim them to be. Draw the diagonals on the ends of the square pieces.

Draw an **octagon** on the end, and continue the corner lines down the wood using your finger as a guide.

Technical stuff

It never hurts to know a little geometry. Get out your old school textbooks; they'll make sense now that you've become a woodworker.

The round wood is already *inside* the square wood. All that needs doing is to cut away the corners in a systematic and thoughtful manner.

An *octagon* has eight equal sides—**A.**

When drawn across to the face, it divides into three parts that are not equal—**A** and **B.**

Making round wood

Our square wood will have to be shaved down to round. Since we are working with flat tools, the easiest way to do this is by cutting off the square corners until no corners remain and the wood seems smooth and round.

In the diagrams above you can see the circle that we are aiming for in the square wood. We start by cutting off the corners to make a figure with eight sides. This is called an *octagon.*

Practice making octagons by drawing a square on a piece of paper.

Draw the diagonals. Set a compass on the corner of the square and strike an arc through the center to intersect each side, as shown in the four diagrams to the right. Join these points to describe an octagon.

An octagon has eight equal sides and, though we will be working free-hand when cutting, it's a good thing to remember this. Too often the tendency is to simply divide each side into three equal parts, making *oval* wood—a nice effect when called for, but not what we're after right now!

Remove the corners of the square with a *drawknife* or *spokeshave.* Remove the resulting corners. You will be able to see and control these smaller facets much easier than the first cuts; so there is no need to pencil them in.

Making a Tiny Chair

Measurements for a tiny chair

Back rails	5¾"	OA (on average)
Front rails	6"	OA
Side rails	7¼"	OA
Rung holes	½"	diameter

Rungs, rails and rounds

Cut some stock pieces—called **billets**—for the rungs. We are using pine for this tiny chair; but if you get ambitious and decide to scale up to build a full-size adult chair, watch that the wood is strong enough.

Look at museum examples or get some books on country furniture. Every piece of wood is different and every person is different; put these two together and you get a lot of variations! What will work for you?

Roughly square the billets, and draw the diagonals at the ends. Put the bit, that you will be using to drill the receiving holes in the legs, onto the center of the ends and give a few turns until the spurs mark a circle. Use these marks to pencil-in lines to cut to as in the step-by-step shown here.

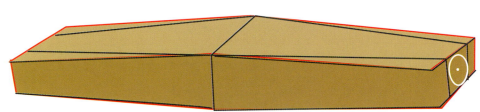

Read the section on legs (pages 120–121) before committing yourself to anything on these two pages!

Rung ends

At each end of the rungs, there is a fairly parallel section, a little larger than the hole in the leg.

Make a **template** or **gauge** from a piece of the hardest wood that you have by drilling holes using the bits that you use for chair-making.

The template can be used to test and form the ends of the rungs as they are being cut. By forcing the rung into the hole, you will compress the pine a little; later, when gluing up, the wood will swell and be tighter.

Seat rails

Notice that the rails that will be *inside* the woven seat are *flattish*—not like the other rungs. This helps the seat be more comfortable. If you find this is too confusing when you are starting out to make chairs, you can make them round—but I think you can do it.

Cut out some billets that are just a bit *thicker* than the diameter of the hole that will receive the seat rung. Mark the ends with a circle centered to one side. Pencil-in half an octagon, and draw down the sides. Remove the corners and round the edge.

Divide the *opposite edge* to the rounding into three parts, and *taper* the top and bottom face. Scoop out the ends and *chamfer* as shown (use your knife bevel-down for this).

Shaving tips

Helps to keep in mind that cutting corners is easier than cutting broad surfaces.

Put your wood in such a position that the corner that you are cutting is uppermost.

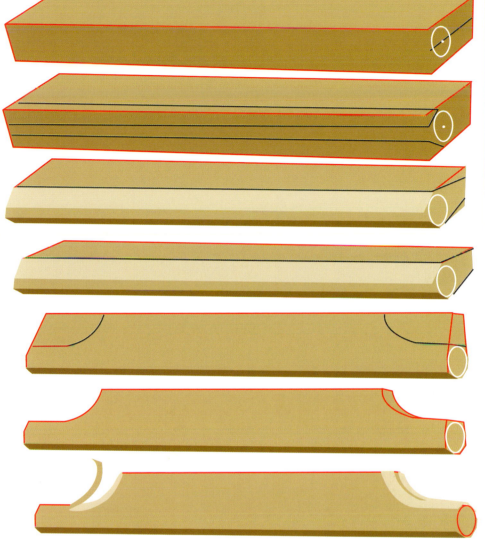

Cutting tapers is easier to control by literally ***cutting corners.***

Not only is the cut narrower, but this way you only have to watch *one line* at a time until the final stages of *flat cutting.*

Making a Tiny Chair

Measurements for a tiny chair

Rung holes	½" diameter
Rung hole depth	¾"
Mortise width	¼" or ⅜"
Mortise depth	½" approximate

More about legs

We are now going to mark the inside of all the legs.

Put the legs together with all the bottom ends in line. A spare piece of wood fixed down to a work surface will help to maintain this important position. Mark the lower parts with a penciled-in centerline.

Take your try square and strike the positions for the rungs and back rails. This drawing gives a fairly good idea of the proportions for these chairs; when you design chairs they will have slightly different proportions and maybe a different number or form of parts, but the principles are the same.

Sequence for preparing the legs

You may notice that the legs in the diagrams below and slightly to the right are already shaved to the **octagonal form.** The legs are easier to mark when they are still square; it's much easier to drill and cut the mortises at the octagonal stage.

A simple depth gauge

A piece of **masking tape** wrapped around the **bit** will give you a rough idea of how deep the drill is into the wood. Measure from the **cutting edges** of the bit, not from the tip of the spur.

This masking-tape depth gauge has a little bonus too— when the depth is reached the tape sweeps the crumbs off the surface letting you know when to stop!

The order of operations

Cut and trim the legs to length and width.
Mark the positions for the rungs and backs.
Shape to octagonal.
Drill holes and cut mortises.
Continue rounding.

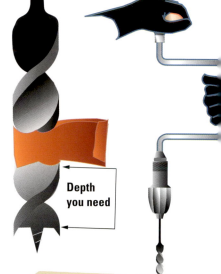

Depth you need

NOTE how the top front rungs, and the corresponding rungs in the back leg, are a fair way down from the top of the front leg. We have to leave room for the side rung, which will be put in between the front top rung and the top of the front leg.

Look again at the pictures on the opening pages of chairs (pages 116–117); this will give you a clearer idea of what's going on.

Take a mortising gauge, and set it to the chisel width—¼" to ⅜" is good for the tiny chair. These joints do not have to take much strain so they can be narrower than the rung-hole diameter.

Drilling

With a brace and bit, drill holes about ¾" deep on the marks made for the rungs. Try to get the hole to be at right angles to the leg in both directions. This is sometimes hard to do; so put your try square or a piece of wood that has a square end next to the bit. This will give you an idea of the correct angle from one side, freeing you to concentrate on keeping the other side cutting squarely.

Holes and mortises

A round hole is just called a hole but a square hole in wood is called a *mortise.*

Round holes are made with a *brace and bit*; mortises are made with *chisels.*

On the following two pages there is more about mortises and how to make them.

90°

90°

Whats going on inside the leg?

When you are working with joints, it's a good idea to visualize what is happening inside the wood as you work. Maybe you're not used to doing this kind of thing; so here is a cross section below to help you.

Notice how the drilled holes stop before the screw center of the bit breaks through. (But if it does, it's not a disaster!)

See how the mortises are not as deep as the drilled holes.

Mortising

As you are well aware by now, a square hole in wood is called a **mortise.** Cutting these holes is called **mortising.**

A sharp chisel is all that is needed for mortising. Some chisels are made specially for making a mortise. **Mortising chisels** are strong and square in section; the squareness helps when cutting because the chisel is less able to twist in the hole. A common **firmer chisel** is fine for what we need here.

Set your **marking gauge** to the width of the chisel you will be using. The corresponding part that goes into the mortise is called a **tenon.** Use the setting for the mortise to mark the tenons.

A marking gauge is a very useful tool to have. The marks made by the points of the marking gauge help to keep the wood from splitting sideways, resulting in a neater job.

Mark the surface to be mortised with the marking gauge set at the width of the chisel. Scribe the ends of the mortise. Place the chisel upright a little way (less than ⅛") in from the scribed mark. The bevel is facing the other end of the mortise.

Strike down with a mallet or the side of your hammer. Repeat at the other end. Move the chisel toward the other end a little, and strike down—not quite as hard as at the ends. Repeat until the cut at the other end is reached. This has established the mortise area. Rub out the crumbs with your thumb.

When you are cutting mortises you will be tempted to turn the chisel sideways sometimes. Resist this temptation! It is very likely that the wood will split. Using the chisel vertically with the grain also leads to trimmed up, sloppy joints. **Don't do it! Don't do it!! Don't do it!!!**

Cross sections of mortise-cutting

The top two rows show a stopped mortise being cut.

You will hear that a mortise is easily made by drilling out the wood first and then trimming the hole. **Don't believe it!** My experience has been that this is the most frustrating way to make a mortise; all trimming, fiddling, and trying not to make a mess—not at all pleasant. **Do it the "hard" way; it's easier.**

For through-mortises, mark the other side of your wood as well, and follow the bottom row of diagrams.

You can do this work **without** a **marking gauge,** but if you can afford it, do get one.

Ask for money for your birthday; I have aquired many tools that way.

Keep the chisel square to the sides of the mortise— do not twist it or turn it!

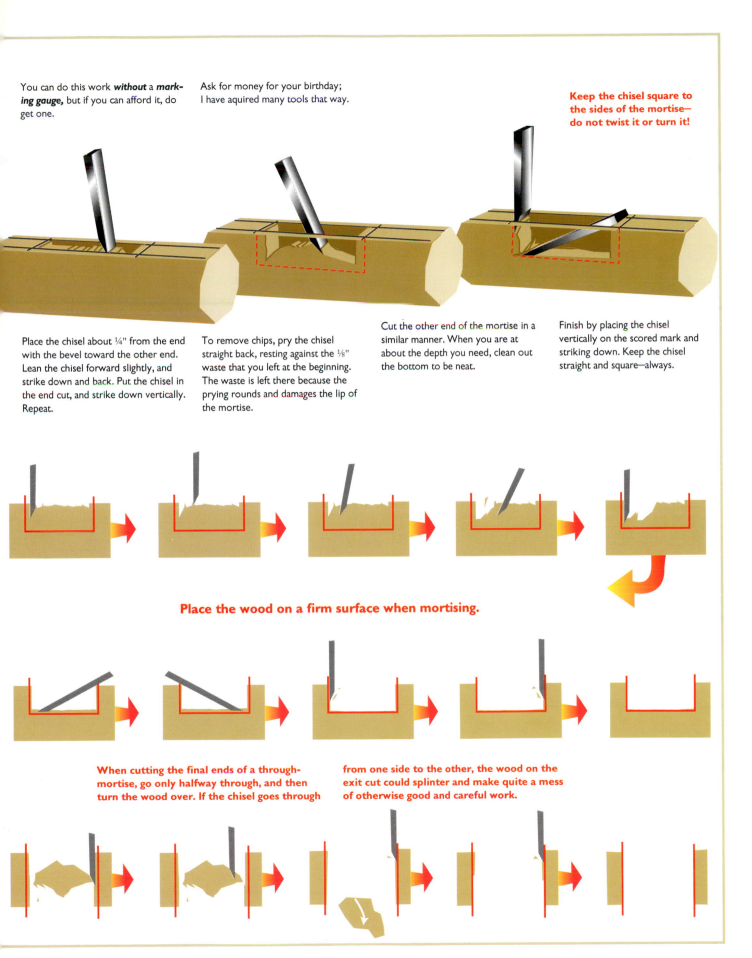

Place the chisel about ¼" from the end with the bevel toward the other end. Lean the chisel forward slightly, and strike down and back. Put the chisel in the end cut, and strike down vertically. Repeat.

To remove chips, pry the chisel straight back, resting against the ⅛" waste that you left at the beginning. The waste is left there because the prying rounds and damages the lip of the mortise.

Cut the other end of the mortise in a similar manner. When you are at about the depth you need, clean out the bottom to be neat.

Finish by placing the chisel vertically on the scored mark and striking down. Keep the chisel straight and square—always.

Place the wood on a firm surface when mortising.

When cutting the final ends of a through-mortise, go only halfway through, and then turn the wood over. If the chisel goes through **from one side to the other, the wood on the exit cut could splinter and make quite a mess of otherwise good and careful work.**

127

Making a Tiny Chair

**Measurements
for a tiny chair**

Back slats   cut from 1"
Angle omega   see plans

First assembly

Now that the rungs and back slats are made we can start to put the whole thing together.

    The chair is made up of two flat parts joined together by rungs on either side. The front frame is wider than the back.

    Carefully push the long rungs into the holes in one of the front legs. Twist them in, but don't wiggle them sideways; wiggling them will make a looser joint— not good! Now take them out, and put them in the other leg. When they are snug, take the other leg and put it on the rungs to form the chair front. Whack it with the palms of your hands to firm it.

    Do the same for the back frame. When putting the slats in, tap them with a mallet or spare piece of wood to help seat them.

The chair back

The shape of the **back slats** is up to you. Have an experimental time. The important part to remember is that the ends have to fit into the mortises. It's very easy to forget this when you're having a great time scooping out the back slats. The lengths of the slats are a little shorter than the rungs; you will recall making the mortises not as deep as the rung holes. The pictures tell all.

Angled drilling

Just as you used a **guide block** for drilling squarely, so you can make blocks to guide you for any angle you need.

The angle will vary from chair to chair; a chalked-up plan is useful to measure from.

Some people may think that my way of working is quite haphazard, but I usually find that a plan drawn with chalk is all I need. A spare wall or piece of board—or even chalking the patio—avoids all those rolled-up papers that are so unruly when you need information.

Angle omega → Ω

90°

Drilling for the side rungs

Lay the **assembled frames** on a flat surface. Strike off the positions for the side rungs. For strength, the front and back rungs are not on the same level as the side rungs. The side rungs are higher up than the cross rungs. The position of the top side rung is between the front top rung and the top of the front leg.

To drill the holes, make a **guide block** to help you keep the correct angle as you drill. Sometimes a friend can help in this operation by saying, "Back a bit and to the left," and so on. The guide block may last a bit longer, though—this drilling can be quite a challenge even to the strongest bonds!

Notice the relationship of the _angle omega_ to the frame. On the front frame it turns in and on the back it turns out.

90°

Ω

Making a Tiny Chair

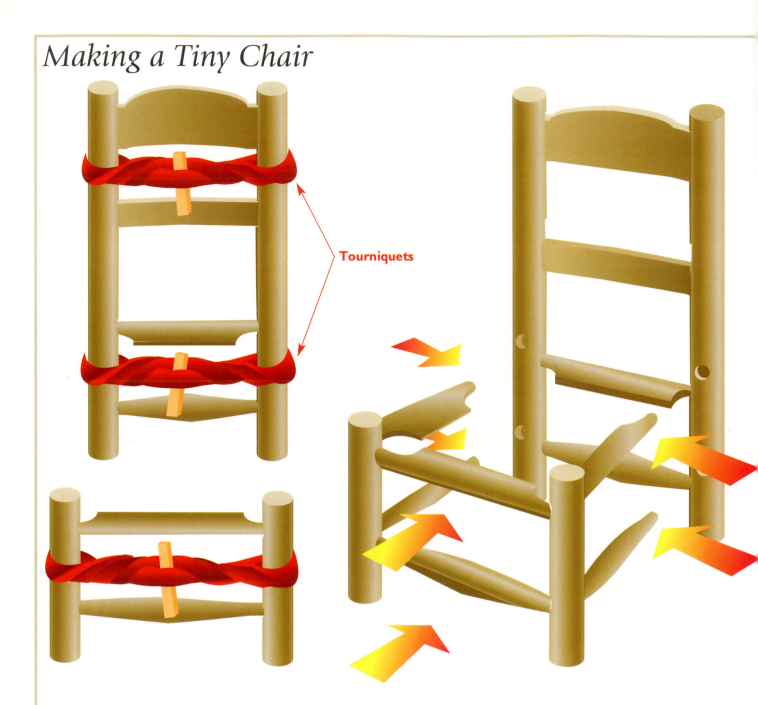

Tourniquets

Gluing

When you are sure that the front and back frames are to your liking, sand them and do any rounding of the tops and bottoms of the legs. Get some good *glue* and put it on the ends of the rungs and slats. Press all the parts into position; maybe a tap or two from a mallet would be good here, too. Wipe off the glue that squeezes out and put on a *tourniquet.*

Clamping the frames

A *tourniquet* is the simplest and cheapest kind of clamp you can get. Get a long strip of cloth about three inches wide. Wind the cloth twice around the object to be glued. Wind a stick of wood inside and tighten up. I find that a pair of tights is great for this job; they are soft and stretchy so you just can't tighten it up too much. If you use string as a tourniquet, put a bit of cardboard from a carton between the string and the wood—enormous pressure is possible when tightening up, and it will damage your work.

Fitting the side rungs

The *side rungs* go in at an angle, so you will need to pinch them in just a little to get them into the holes in the back legs.

You cant force a cat

Be patient when putting the chair together; it can be frustrating, but be quiet and be patient. Talk to your chair quietly. Say things gently, like "That's it, come on, this will soon be over," or "I'm finding this a bit hard to do, perhaps I need to check something that's causing this problem."

Talk to your work as you would talk to a *cat.* Treat your work as you would a *cat.* Expect from your work what you expect from a cat. Force and rough behavior are not the way.

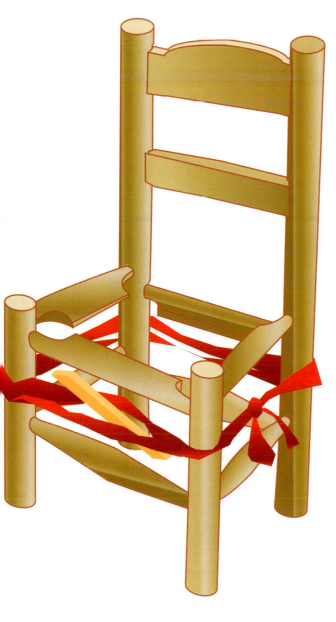

More gluing

Put a **tourniquet** around the whole chair after gluing up the side rungs and putting them in place.

There is a possibility that the chair will not sit squarely on the ground—now is the time to push it down into shape. If the chair is madly out of shape, don't expect to fix it when gluing—but little adjustments are possible.

Painting the chair

Any color is nice for a chair, or, if you like the wood color, just leave it.

Pine and cedar will become darker with exposure to light. A healthy wipe-over with a rag soaked in boiled linseed oil and a good rubdown are all that's needed for an oil finish. Shellac works well on small jobs to give the wood a slight shine.

Some Simple Chairs—Seat-Weaving with Fibers

Vegetable **fibers** of just about any kind can be used to weave a seat for a chair or stool.

Rushes are the most familiar vegetable matter for this job; they have been used for hundreds of years. I read once that I needed a special kind of reed to do this work and so I went out and got a load of ordinary, bullrush-type reeds that were growing beside the road across from my house. Dried them. Used them. They were great! So much for special reeds.

Living in the town, as I do now, can be a problem when it comes to getting fibers for weaving seats; but there is a great supply right under our noses—cotton.

Go to the rag bag, Goodwill, or charity shop and get an old pair of blue jeans! They don't even have to be blue; any color is fine.

A while ago I bought some curtains at a yard sale, cheap, that I thought were wonderful—nobody else did. They are now the seat of a rocking chair.

Cut the cloth into strips about two inches wide and fold the edges in so that no threads hang out. Weave as the drawings here show how. Finish up with a tack in the back rung.

You will find that the rows are sometimes difficult to keep in parallel lines. Fake it! Nobody is going to come and measure it; if it's uncomfortable, though—fix it.

While we're on the subject, here's a very important rule that helps you stay disciplined—**don't make things just for show; they have got to work.** Any fool can make something that's just for looking at!

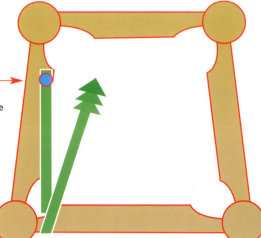

Start here
Tack in the end of the first weaving strip to the rung. Don't pull hard; just be firm. Keep up this firm pulling throughout the seat.

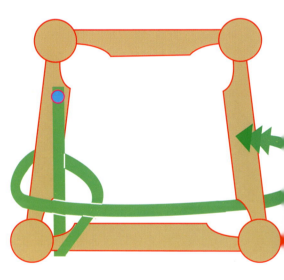

Joining strips of cloth
Make a slit in the end of the piece you are weaving with and in the piece to join to it.

Slip the end of the weaving piece into the hole in the new piece until it's past the hole. Put the end of the new piece into the hole in the weaving piece and pull it back. Proceed. Hard to describe, easy to do—see the picture.

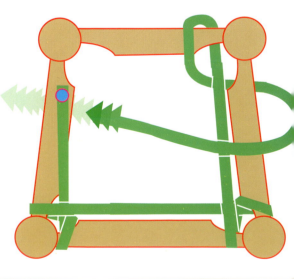

Chair frames are generally wider in the front for strength. Therefore the side rungs are angled. Weaving runs square and so you may, just like people for hundreds of years, have difficulty with the strips' not being parallel. Something you will not notice until you get near the middle of the seat, and then it's too late! There is a very simple solution to this.

To keep the strips parallel, **pencil a line** on the front rung, square with the back leg. This can be done by just putting a square plank on the frame and eyeballing it. The line doesn't have to be very accurate. Start weaving by putting in a few strands that only go around three sides. When you reach the pencil line, weave all the way around.

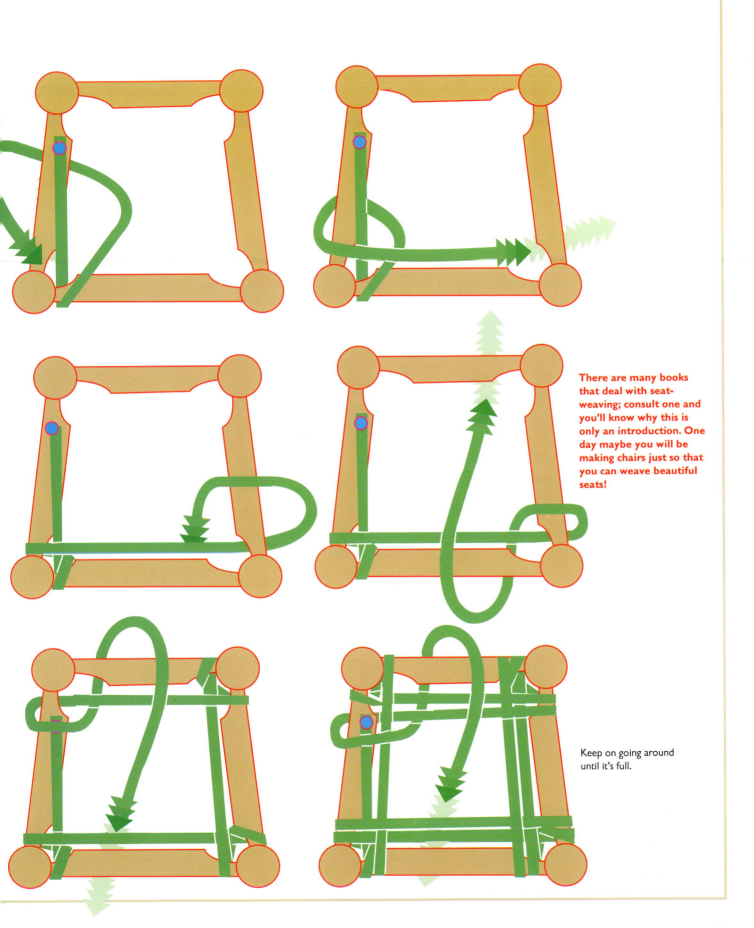

There are many books that deal with seat-weaving; consult one and you'll know why this is only an introduction. One day maybe you will be making chairs just so that you can weave beautiful seats!

Keep on going around until it's full.

Making an Armchair

Chairs with something to rest your arms on are called **armchairs.** It is very simple to modify your chair-making ways to bring an armchair into being.

This armchair is made in the same way as other simple chairs except that it has front legs that are longer. At the tops of the legs are **round tenons** that are made by sawing around the shoulders and chiseling away the waste. Another way to do this is to drill a hole in the top of the leg and insert a **dowel** (handmade or bought). Drill a hole in the back leg to take the tenon at the end of the arm, when you are drilling for rungs.

When gluing up, leave the arm-gluing until you have woven the seat; not having the arms in the way makes it less frustrating.

Seat

Cloth or rushes can be used to weave the seat; but something fun for this rugged little piece is a **babiche seat.**

Babiche is an Algonkian/French Canadian word for strips of raw-hide such as you find in snowshoe fillings. Rawhide is sometimes hard to find, but you can use the weaving patterns (on pages 136–137) to weave any long strip of cord or cloth for some very pretty effects.

The big advantage of rawhide is that it tightens as it dries; if you use cloth or cord you will have to tighten it yourself.

Growing

This may be a bit small for today's kids, so make the chair bigger by increasing the lengths an inch or so. When using pine, the parts can stay the same diameters until you get midway between this and full size—then boost them a bit.

Eyeballing is important here—make it look right.

Research

There are a lot of startlingly inexpensive plastic chairs for children on the market these days. Take a rule and get some measurements from them. Books about North American antique furniture have lots of chair pictures; they are great inspiration.

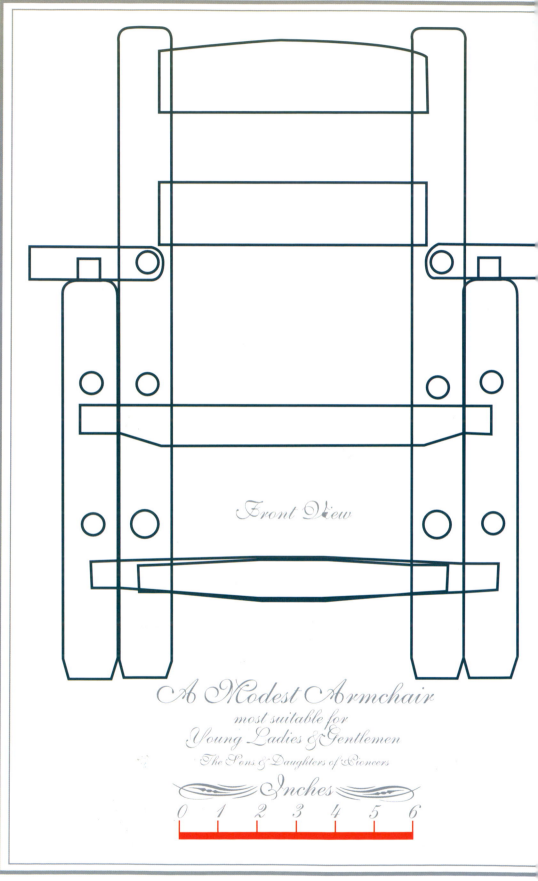

Front View

A Modest Armchair
most suitable for
Young Ladies & Gentlemen
The Sons & Daughters of Pioneers

Inches

0   1   2   3   4   5   6

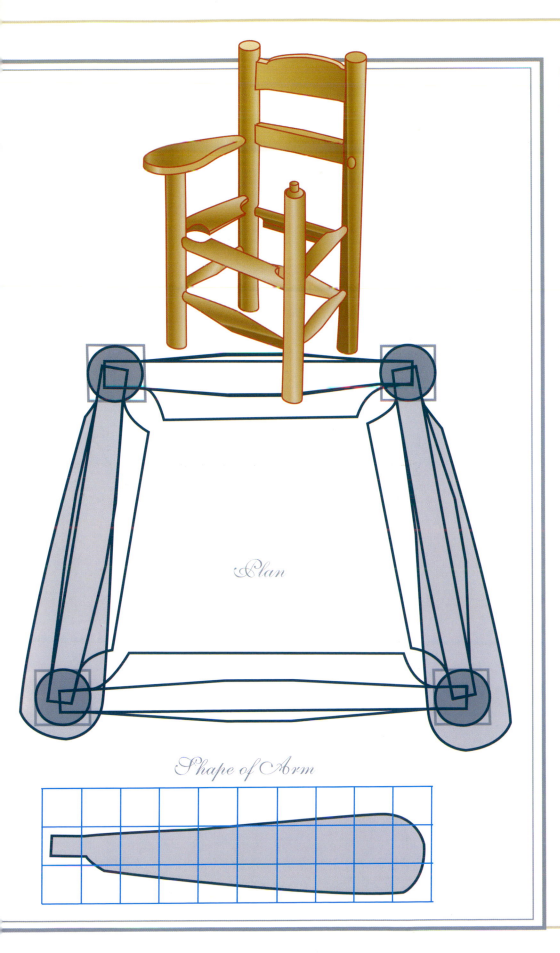

Plan

Shape of Arm

Babiche seats

Rawhide is the skin of an animal that has had the hair removed. Nothing more.

In its dry state, rawhide is light grayish brown in color or sometimes white. Sometimes you can buy deer hides from taxidermists to make your own rawhide. Don't get anything that has been treated in any way. Salt is okay; but nothing else. If you know some people who hunt, you can often get the hide from them, if you tell them what you are doing.

Take the hide with hair on it and soak it in water for a couple or three days; the hair will slip off. To soak the hide, a big garbage bag is the simplest container; use a clean trash can if you have one. When you remove the hair, take off any fat from the flesh side, too.

Nail the cleaned hide on a shed or large board, or make a frame like in the movies and string out the hide to stretch and dry. A dry hide will last for years and years; it will not deteriorate at all if it's kept dry.

Take the hide down and roll it up until you need it. Cut a disk from the rawhide about 12" across. Cut a spiral strip about ⅜" wide. Soak in clean water for a couple of days and it's ready to use. Do not forget about the rawhide soaking—the longer it soaks, the more it stinks!

Take the soaked rawhide from the water and pull it through your hands to stretch it. A strip about seven yards long will be needed for the armchair.

Cutting a strip

Deer rawhide can be cut with scissors or tin snips. Thicker hides may need a surgical blade or utility knife.

Some Simple Chairs—Babiche-Weaving

Whether you're weaving with moose hide, raccoon, garden twine, or silk pajamas torn into strips, the secret is that strips going in one direction always do the same thing when they meet another strip.

In the diagram above observe the three strips **A, B,** & **C.**

The strips are travelling in different directions.

A goes over **B** and under **C.**
B goes over **C** and under **A.**
C goes over **A** and under **B.**
Always.

Twist and turn your work no matter which way— this rule still applies.

As the weaving progresses you will start to see the X shapes appear. Learn to recognize them (in all directions); they will help you decide on which side to put a strand.

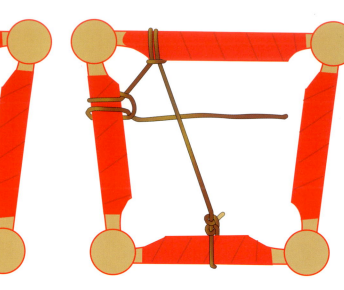

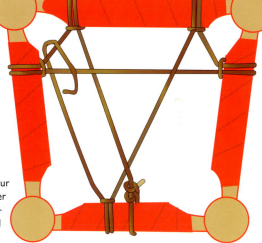

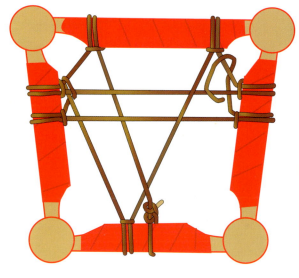

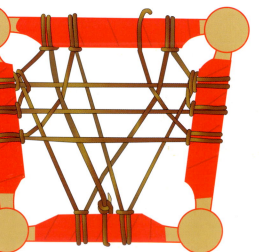

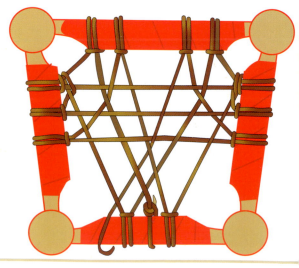

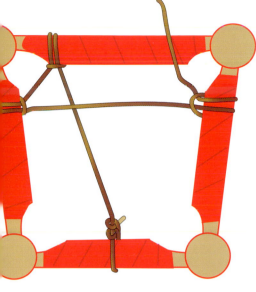

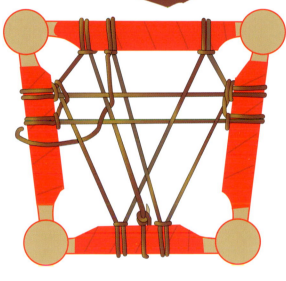

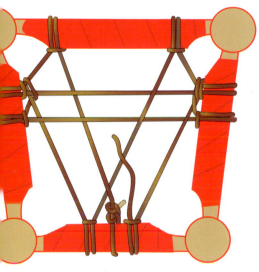

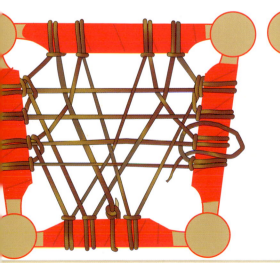

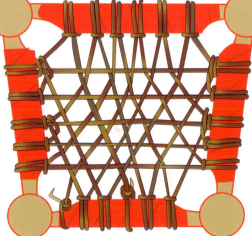

Before starting

Get some paper and a pencil and draw the path of the rawhide weaving. Don't worry about the over and under; just try remembering which side to go to next. Practice on paper until you feel pretty good about where the weaving goes. The over and under is then the only thing to recall.

Flannel

The Ojibwe used to wrap the sides of their *agimuk* (snowshoes) with red flannel. I find it quite attractive and so I always put it on my chairs. You can, too; any color is nice—if you like it. The flannel makes it difficult to slip the rawhide along the rungs, so be sure of your spacing or try at first with just bare rungs.

Joining strips

Often the rawhide strip is not long enough, and working with too long a strip is not efficient; join the ends as shown here.

Finishing

Rawhide works best if it's just left to dry. Varnish doesn't do a thing for it except make it look very flashy when young and sadly shabby in its old age. I think it's smart not to varnish rawhide. **P.S.** If you are lucky enough to get some snowshoes without varnish, leave them that way, I beseech you! Varnishing snowshoes renders them less efficient.

The varnish traps water that is forced into the rawhide through the cracks that form in the varnish the moment that you use them. The shoes become more and more soggy as the winter progresses. All snowshoe filling takes in a little water in use, but it can evaporate or freeze dry when resting; the varnish stops the water from getting out.

Rawhide has a natural spring to it; this spring helps the snowshoer walk for longer periods without tiring. Varnish stops the rawhide from springing and turns the snowshoe into a lump of stuff at the end of your leg that gets heavier and heavier as winter progresses and it takes on more and more water, etc.

Don't varnish snowshoes!

Making a Rocking Chair

With a little more work you can make your chair into an even more confidence-building project—go for the **rockers!**

Marking up

Take the wood that you are going to use for the rocker blades—1" pine is good for a little chair—and lay it across the upturned legs of the chair. Draw on the thickness with a pencil.

Take the chair apart, and scribe a line about an inch and a half all around each leg. Draw the lines from the bottoms of the legs straight down to cross this line. You have now marked the **open mortises** that will house the rockers.

Saw down the mortise lines to the scribed line.

Chop out the waste with a chisel.

Put the chair back together when all four legs are cut. Insert the board that you will be using for the rockers. Draw the arcs as shown; the back end of the rocker is a straight tangent to the main curve, which will stop the chair from going over backwards quite as easily. Cut, chamfer, and shape to your desire.

To join the blade to the leg, draw, bore, and treenail the parts together.

Marking the blade

When the joints at the end of the leg are cut, put the board for the rocker in position. Draw the shape of the rocker on the wood. The center of the main curve (the part that touches the floor) will make a fast or slow rocking chair depending on how high or low you put the center.

I have no formula for this, just eyeballing and practice—and of course trying to be scientific, which can work, sometimes.

Marking the legs

Put the rocker wood on the bottom of the legs of the upturned chair.

Pencil or strike the thickness onto the leg ends.

Take these lines down to a line drawn around the legs that is at the depth that the rocker will be seated into the legs.

Sawing out the legs

Saw accurately down to the line.

Leg ends finesse

Chamfer off the ends of the legs—the **cheeks** of the mortise—and around the mortise to remove the edges that would be easily damaged.

See how this makes it look better even though it's done for purely practical reasons? Does the answer to the "chicken and egg" riddle lie here?

Chiseling out the legs

With the leg on a firm surface, and the saw cuts straight up and down, place the chisel on the line and strike down with a mallet.

Place the chisel on the end grain about as far down as your first strike went into the wood, and strike in.

A slight tap should do it. A piece of the wood will come out.

Repeat these two moves until halfway through.

Turn the leg over and repeat the chiseling.

Grain

Grain

Grain

Grain

Grain

Grain

Grain

Draw-boring pulls the joint close and snug; it can be used with any mortise-and-tenon joint if the tenon is long enough.

Draw-boring

You may have often seen furniture with dowels near the joints. Generally this is just fake, done for effect.

When done properly this method of fastening wood together is not simply a hole drilled straight through with a dowel inserted—and it certainly isn't just some feel-good decoration! *Draw-boring* actually draws the joint tight.

Make a ***treenail*** from a piece of wood harder than that used for the chair (see page 52 for something more about treenails and treen).

Insert the thin end into the leg hole so that it also passes through the hole in the rocker blade and out the leg hole on the other side.

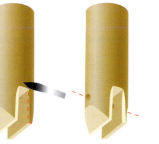

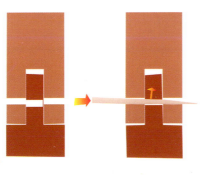

Drill a ¼" hole **X** through the *cheeks* that you have just made . Insert the rocker blade and seat it as firmly into position as you can.

Put the ¼" auger bit that was used to drill the cheeks into the hole on one side and push down a little, marking the rocker blade with the auger center. Withdraw the rocker. Observe the center mark that you have just made. Directly below it about ¹⁄₁₆" down, mark another center **Y,** and drill it with a ¼" bit.

Be careful in doing this, because an oak treenail will drive right through the softer wood if it misses the hole!

Trim off the bits of the treenail sticking out on both sides.

Once you've put your draw-bored joints together, it's pretty tricky to get them apart again; so wait to do this job last.

X

Y

SHARPENING

Why do we always put off sharpening? Even in this book it's almost an afterthought. Maybe it's because there's a right way, a wrong way, and a real answer to the problem of bluntness. It's not difficult to do and it's quite satisfying; and it's certainly no big deal. Maybe it's because some people have made it into a big deal and mystery. Make it is a mystery and you'll make it a *misery!*

Sharpening is just making an edge real skinny but not so much that it will break off when you push it into something. Sharpening is making a wedge-shaped edge that will be able to catch in the wood and split a piece off in a very controlled way.

Stones

Nothing happens suddenly—and so with sharpening stones. Start with a rough stone, then use a medium, next a fine, then a smooth, and finally a piece of leather or the palm of your hand.

The different kinds of rock that are made into sharpening stones all have their own names—names that I can never remember and neither need you. It might help, though, to get a little knowedgable when you set out to purchase stones; but after that it doesn't matter. Read a few catalogues. Go to the library; read some books.

I bought a set in a box some years ago that have worked well for me. They are small, about four inches by two, but that's plenty big enough. Stones are expensive but you can often get them cheap at junk stores, used furniture stores, and yard sales.

Most woodworking tools have two wedge shapes on their business end; the main bevel ground on, and the sharpened bevel. The **ground bevel** gets the shaft down to shape ready for the **sharpening bevel.** One rarely needs to do anything with the ground bevel at our level of work; the sharpened bevel needs some care and consideration. The back of bevel-sharpened tools is flat, flat, flat!!!

DULL White edge
Sharpening bevel
Ground bevel

Chisels

Make sure that you keep a **constant angle** when pushing the chisel forward. The tendency is to roll your hands; but you must always keep the tool firmly at the same angle. The return stroke is light—no pressure. Always keep the back flat—never lift it up at an angle—if you want an efficient tool.

Once you have found this angle, keep it in your head and hands!

Burrs

A **burr** is the edge of the blade that has become so thin that it bends over instead of wearing off. Feel the burr by rubbing your finger away from the edge. The burr will become a wire edge as you stone both sides.

Fixing dull edges

When an edge becomes dull, it reflects light. Hold the blade up, and look at the edge; if you see a white line, the blade needs a little sharpening. Even one small speck of white will effect its cutting efficiency.

Put a little oil on the stone. Automobile engine oil is okay to use—10W30 is a good weight.

Oil Blip **Blade** **Stone**

Wire edge

Wearing away the metal with a stone causes the edge to become so very thin that it can take no more pressure; instead of wearing away, it bends over. This bent-over edge is called a **burr.**

Wire edge

Take the blade for sharpening, and put it on the stone in the oil patch. The sharpening angle must be parallel to the stone. To discover the correct angle, when you put the blade into the oil, change the angle until a little blip of oil squeezes out from beneath the sharpening edge. This tells you that you are holding the tool at the correct angle.

Blade **Stone**

By stoning the other side of the blade, this burr becomes a thin piece of metal stuck on the end of the tool by very little other than its own willpower. This is called a **wire edge;** and just as wire will snap if you bend it backwards and forwards enough, so we can remove the wire edge by bending it back and forward. This is **stropping;** watch a barber doing it to his razors. Stropping also removes stone marks for an even keener edge. An old leather belt works well for this.

Jigs

Small blades such as spokeshave blades can be tricky to hold while sharpening. A couple of pieces of wood screwed together can help.

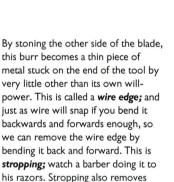

Holding the tool at the correct angle, push the blade firmly forward, maintaining the angle.

Do this a few times; then turn the blade over and, with the back flat on the stone, push the blade firmly forward a few times.

If the blade is very dull, start with the coarsest stone and then go to the medium, etc. Do the same movements on each stone. If the blade is just a little dull, then just a touch-up on the finest stone and a strop will be enough.

Drawknives

All blades that have a **double-bevel edge** are sharpened in similar manner. Bevel on one side, flat on the back.

Drawknives are a little more awkward but nevertheless are treated in the same way as *chisels*.

Blade

Stone

Blade

Stone

Axes and hatchets

These two traditional settlers' tools are usually shown in the movies being sharpened with a big ol' grind stone. Who, nowadays, has one of those? Use a file. Hardware stores sell a file called an **axe file** or a "farmer's friend"; smooth on one side and rough on the other, it's a good thing to have, though any medium-to-fine file works well if that's what you have.

The natural tendency is to file **away** from the edge, but you should file **into the edge**. Get a good ground bevel and then put on a sharpening bevel. Flat-file the back.

Augers

The soft metal of auger bits can be sharpened with a file. Have a really good look at the auger, and know what you are doing before you start.

Augers have two sets of cutting edges; each set has two parts. File the horizontal cutting edges in the direction shown. File the inside of the spurs, lightly. **Do not file the outside of the spurs.**

Do not file any of the parts **colored red** in the diagrams.

Auger files have teeth only on the flats at one end and on the edges at the other end. If you can find an auger file, they are really good to use; **needle files** are more plentiful and work well, too.

Wagon or center bits

Almost the same as augers, though sometimes the point gets dull—and in this case it's all right to touch it up a bit; keep it symetrical, though.

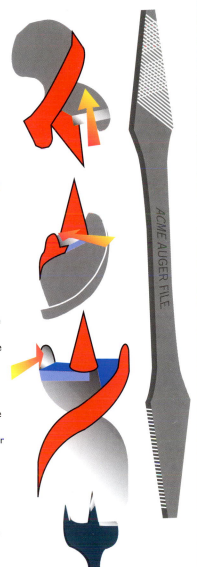

Bye for
NOW

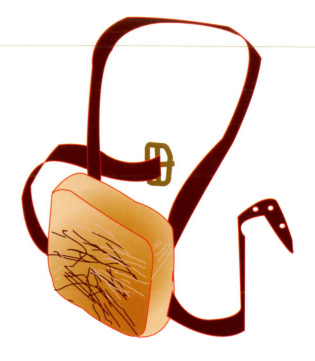

Either you go toward something or you go away from it. You can't go parallel. Sometimes paths cross and a good feeling comes from that. Like the time I needed something to help me put some tenons on some spokes and I "designed" my breast bib. The very next week I was looking through a tool book, and there was the same shaped bib made by someone in 1649. Well I'm not alone, I thought, as I wondered who that person was who made it so long ago; food, family and friends, sadness and joy, all in one piece of wood. Hardly considered, in its day, to be anything of worth.

No matter what we do it's going to affect somebody or something. *Nothing* is impossible. If you make a box, you make its shadow, too. No matter where we step, some world, small to us, but not to those that live there, gets affected in some way. But we have to move around and do things; that is our nature.

My nature seems to be to learn. My nature is the nature of woodworking; the quiet pleasures of crafting by hand. I like doing things quietly and I like thinking. Not the kind of thinking that gets you all worked up and fanatical, because then you're gonna go out and stomp on things deliberately. Some people make a real nuisance of themselves because they think that everybody should be like them and that their's is the one and only way. There is no one way to do anything. If you've done a lot of the things we've talked about in this book, I think you'll know what I mean. Consideration.

Index

Try as I might I can never seem to measure something using a ruler and then cut it to fit. Something always seems to go wrong! Yet I can eyeball and cut it to fit right on. I think it has something to do with the natural space and cultures that we live in. Be that as it may, the problem is that different cultures have different feelings about some things, and these have been converted into measurements. I have worked in both metric and imperial and it's kinda like being bilingual. Measurement is like a language in that you only need it when your want to communicate with another person or a machine; so don't make a big deal out of it, I say. I've been unable to avoid using some standard measurements in this book, so I've put here a kind of measurement phrase book. It'll be handy until you get used to just reaching out for the right size tool that you know will do what you want.

Did I ever tell you about the time I wondered about how those old guys a hundred years ago did such accurate work? Well, I got an old book and looked it up it said "After you have measured out your stuff. Check all dimensions and then hold the piece against the place it is intended to fit, to see that it is correct." Lovely!

Metric Equivalents

inches	mm	cm
⅛	3	0.3
¼	6	0.6
⅜	10	1.0
½	13	1.3
⅝	16	1.6
¾	19	1.9
⅞	22	2.2
1	25	2.5
1¼	32	3.2
1½	38	3.8
1¾	44	4.4
2	51	5.1
2½	64	6.4
3	76	7.6
3½	89	8.9
4	102	10.2
4½	114	11.4
5	127	12.7
6	152	15.2
7	178	17.8
8	203	20.3
9	229	22.9
10	254	25.4
11	279	27.9
12	305	30.5

inches	mm	cm
13	330	33.0
14	356	35.6
15	381	38.1
16	406	40.6
17	432	43.2
18	457	45.7
19	483	48.3
20	508	50.8
21	533	53.3
22	559	55.9
23	584	58.4
24	610	61.0
25	635	63.5
26	660	66.0
27	686	68.6
28	711	71.1
29	737	73.7
30	762	76.2
31	787	78.7
32	813	81.3
33	838	83.8
34	864	86.4
35	889	88.9
36	914	91.4
37	940	94.0
38	965	96.5
39	991	99.1
40	1016	101.6

inches	mm	cm
41	1041	104.1
42	1067	106.7
43	1092	109.2
44	1118	111.8
45	1143	114.3
46	1168	116.8
47	1194	119.4
48	1219	121.9
49	1245	124.5
50	1270	127.0

inches	feet	m
12	1	0.305
24	2	0.610
36	3	0.914
48	4	1.22
60	5	1.52
72	6	1.83
84	7	2.13
96	8	2.44
108	9	2.74
120	10	3.05
180	15	4.57
240	20	6.10
300	25	7.62
360	30	9.15

Conversion Factors

1 mm	=	0.039 inch	1 inch = 25.4 mm = 0.025 m	mm	= millimeter
1 m	=	3.28 feet	1 foot = 304.8 mm = 0.305 m	cm	= centimeter
1 m²	=	10.8 square feet	1 square foot = 0.09 m²	m	= meter
1 liter	=	0.26 gallons	1 gallon = 3.8 liters	m²	= square meter